AUTHOR'S STATEMENT

This book is not about relationships failing. It is about authority being violated.

An entanglement forms when something is taken that was never lawfully offered. When presence, peace, obedience, emotional labor, or identity is extracted rather than freely given. These knots are not obvious at first. They do not announce themselves as bondage. They form quietly, through repeated concessions, until movement becomes restricted and peace becomes conditional.

Entanglements are not always dramatic. They are often polite. They often wear the language of love, duty, unity, or concern.

But what God joins brings rest. What He did not authorize produces strain. An entanglement is an illegal knot formed when access, control, or regulation is taken without God-given authority.

Illegal knots bind what should remain voluntary. They restrict what God left free, and they demand what covenant did not authorize. They are maintained not by agreement, but by pressure.

This book is not about cutting people off. It is about *loosening* what God never tied.

Table of Contents

ENTANGLEMENTS ARE ILLEGAL KNOTS 5

4 MAJOR TYPES OF ENTANGLEMENTS 7

SIGNS OF ENTANGLEMENT 13

WHAT MAKES A KNOT ILLEGAL......................... 17

HOW DID THIS HAPPEN? 19

KNOTS & ENERGY 26

ENTANGLEMENT VERSUS HEALTHY INTERDEPENDENCE 28

NOT AUTHORIZED.. 33

ILLEGAL KNOTS & HUMAN RELATIONSHIPS 37

RECOGNIZING YOU'RE ENTANGLED 41

ENTANGLEMENTS VS SOUL TIES 54

IDENTITY ENTANGLEMENTS................................ 57

MENTORSHIP ENTANGLEMENTS......................... 63

SPIRITUAL ENTANGLEMENTS.............................. 68

FORGET ME KNOTS 73

THREE PRIMARY CATEGORIES OF ENTANGLEMENT 75

THE 5-THREADS OF ENTANGLEMENT 85

COUNTERFEIT CORDS 92

PROPHETIC & SENSITIVE PEOPLE GET ENTANGLED EASILY 101

DREAM KNOTS	108
SPIRIT SPOUSE – SPIRIT CHILDREN	117
OPPORTUNISTIC ONES	119
ENTANGLEMENTS BY DARK METHODS	121
FINANCIAL ENTANGLEMENTS	126
ENTANGLEMENTS IN LEADERSHIP & MINISTRY	130
PROPHETIC ENTANGLEMENT	140
WHEN THE LEADER IS ENTANGLED	142
Dear Reader	143
Prayerbooks by this author	144
Prayer Manuals	145
Other books by this author	146

ISBN: 978-1-971933-09-2

Paperback Version

Copyright 2026, Dr. Marlene Miles

All rights reserved. No part of this book may be reproduced, distributed, or transmitted by any means or in any means including photocopying, recording or other electronic or mechanical methods without prior written permission of the publisher except in the case of brief publications or critical reviews.

ENTANGLEMENTS:

Illegal Knots Limiting Your Life

by Dr. Marlene Miles

Freshwater Press 2026

Freshwaterpress9@gmail.com

All Scripture references taken from the KJV of the Holy Bible, unless otherwise indicated.

ENTANGLEMENTS ARE ILLEGAL KNOTS

Entanglements are illegal spiritual knots. They restrict movement God never intended to limit. They demand access God never granted. And they require pressure where love would have sufficed.

Entanglements are about jurisdiction. Something can feel normal, familiar, or even loving, and still be unauthorized. Scripture is clear that authority is not vague or emotional; it is assigned, limited, and accountable.

Entanglements are not as clean as *soul ties*, and they are not as obvious as bondage. They are *sticky*, *messy*, *interwoven*--, complicated, and *hard to separate*. They are threads crossing that shouldn't cross. Taboo connections connecting but they shouldn't. Information flowing where it shouldn't flow. They are energies and intentions intertwining. Think of them as people tied together by circumstances more than covenant and situations that coil around progress.

Entanglements are invisible knots that steal clarity, Peace, and purpose.

Entanglements are dangerous because they have an emotional pull. They blur discernment and distract people from their assignment. They hijack focus, introduce atmospheric fog, and create guilt loops. They can even make a person protect another person that they don't even owe. They steal time, clarity, and identity without ever announcing themselves.

Entanglements are spiritual traffic jams. They behave as delays and obstructions and weights, even though all weights are not heavy; some are just severely tangled.

An entanglement is a *knot in the unseen realm. It is the result of t*wo or more lives overlapping in ways God did not authorize, creating confusion instead of clarity, drain instead of direction, noise instead of knowing. It's not a relationship, covenant or a soul tie. An entanglement is a cross-wiring of boundaries, emotions, expectations, and spiritual access.

Where soul ties bond, entanglements snare. There is no mutual agreement in an entanglement; a person is just caught. Entanglements don't just happen. Someone is usually pressing for a closeness the other person did not intend to give. Where mutual attachments can soothe, entanglements drain. Where real relationships define, entanglements blur. They are subtle, silent, and spiritually disruptive.

Entanglements are floating. They are invisible until illuminated. They are intricate and often formed by a series of small interactions. Entanglements seem powerful, but are fragile once you pull the right cord.

4 MAJOR TYPES OF ENTANGLEMENTS

There are four types of entanglements: Emotional, Situational, Intellectual/ Identity, and Spiritual.

Emotional Entanglements come from oversharing, trauma-bonding, dependency disguised as closeness, Friendships where one person is the therapist. Feeling WAY more than the relationship level justifies

Emotional Entanglements happen when people share too much, too fast, and with the wrong person. Symptoms include emotional investment that make no sense, rollercoaster dynamic, and or hyper-awareness of someone who doesn't matter. Feeling responsible for *their* feelings. Anxiety if they withdraw. Emotional Entanglements form when vulnerability gets ahead of Wisdom. They show up as hypersensitivity to someone's moods, feeling "connected" to someone you've never been in covenant with. Emotional entanglements FEEL like closeness but function like confusion.

How can you tell? Your emotions move faster than the relationship reality.

Situational Entanglements aren't emotional at all. They are *circumstantial traps*. You work together, for example. You travel together. You serve together. You're in the same small church. You go to school together. They look at you, with *that look*. You're in a group chat together. You bonded through crisis or pressure.

How can you tell? The situation created false closeness.

Situational Entanglements are created by shared work, shared trauma, shared pressure, even if you are on a shared mission. Shared community. These combinations create a *false bond* that mimics closeness that evaporates outside the situation. **Situational Entanglements** can occur when proximity + pressure creates a false bond.

This can happen at work, in ministry, at church, in a crisis, in a community, or even in family systems, During stressful seasons. When the situation ends, the "connection" dissolves…yet the residue remains.

Spiritual Entanglements

This kind of entanglement blindsides a lot of Christians. They can be created through shared secrets--, people without the *spirit of counseling* are not good choices to share your secrets with; they will mishandle it by using it to their own benefit, or they will blab and tell your business to others. Shared rituals, even those that seem benign, can create a spiritual entanglement. Shared spiritual language such as prayer partnerships formed too fast can lead to entanglement. You need to be wise and discerning when you agree to pray with anyone. You must know who they are, that they're really saved, that their motives are pure, and they are praying to the same God that you're praying to. Praying opens your spirit up and you don't want to be in the room or in an environment with anyone who is not of God while you are in prayer, worship or any other spiritual state. Yes, there are charlatans out here and even in the church.

Prophetic dependence can create a spiritual entanglement. Always taking counsel from someone who is not the Holy Spirit can dull your discernment as well as quench or grieve the Spirit of God if you are not listening to what He's saying to you, but instead calling 'a friend'. Additionally, you could be taking counsel from the wrong person.

How do you know? People who shouldn't influence your spiritual atmosphere, do. Some symptoms may be: disrupted sleep, preoccupation, or your discernment going offline.

My yoke is easy, and My burden is light. (Matthew 11) Any yoke that tightens under rest, autonomy, or obedience to God is not Christ's yoke, regardless of who placed it. Spiritual entanglements are the most dangerous. They are formed by prayer partnerships, Prophetic dependence. Shared secrets. "Covering" that God didn't authorize. Manipulative counsel. Signs of spiritual energy exchange, or confusion after interacting with them, fog, feeling spiritually drained. I spoke to a "prophet" by phone who was highly recommended by a prayer partner. In no more than three phone calls I realized that after talking with this person, even for 10 or 15 minutes, afterward I felt flat, spiritually drained. I had to stop immediately, so I did. Period. I don't believe an entanglement had been placed, but it felt like pre-entanglement territory.

False prophetic dependence is a form of spiritual entanglement. It is dangerous not because it's dramatic, but because of what it replaces. Psychics, horoscopes, astrology, weekly calls for "direction" is not merely curiosity or entertainment when it becomes dependence. It becomes an outsourcing of agency and discernment. That is the entanglement.

What makes it an entanglement and not just a belief? An entanglement forms when a person cannot decide without consulting an external source. Direction is sought outside conscience, Wisdom, prayer, and counsel. Anxiety increases when the source is unavailable. The source becomes authoritative, not advisory. The person feels "off" or unsafe without guidance from it. At that point, it's not information-seeking, it's attachment.

It's called *prophetic dependence,* even when it's false, because functionally, it mirrors prophetic abuse. Signs are feelings or needs such as: *Tell me what will happen. Tell me what choice to make. Tell me who I am.*

Tell me what's coming. Tell me what to fear. Whether it's a psychic hotline, astrology charts, tarot, horoscopes, energy readers, constant "signs" interpretation, …the role is the same. The person has surrendered *decision-making authority*. That's the core issue.

This kind of dependence is dangerous because it erodes personal responsibility, dulls discernment, creates learned helplessness. It also replaces Wisdom and the Holy Spirit with prediction, trains people to avoid accountability. It feeds rather than resolving anxiety. Spiritually speaking, it substitutes trust. Not everyone involved believes in demons. Not everyone is afraid. Many are simply *uncertain* and looking for reassurance, but reassurance that must be continually purchased or consulted is not Peace; it's bondage by dependency.

The Biblical problem is that Scripture consistently warns against divination, fortune-telling, omens, signs-as-guidance, *familiar spirits* and any other voice replacing God's Voice.

Guidance was never meant to be externalized that way. The Biblical model is Wisdom, counsel, prayer, conscience, responsibility, growth in discernment. Any system that requires you to repeatedly consult it in order to live cannot be a source of freedom. Prophetic dependence, true or false, becomes an entanglement when it replaces discernment rather than sharpening it.

That covers abusive prophecy, psychic dependence, horoscope fixation, astrology-based decision making. All without drama. Occasional curiosity ≠ entanglement. Habitual reliance = entanglement. It's not about the *thing*, *it*'s about the function it serves.

False prophetic dependence is real. It functions exactly like unhealthy spiritual authority. It creates entanglement through reliance, not fear. **Intellectual / Identity Entanglements** sneak up quietly. You got connected through purpose or creative work. Or connected through ministry vision. Business dreams, ministry calling or gifting are other ways these connections form.

How do you know? Your sense of self starts tying to someone else's role, opinion, or approval.

DISCERNMENT QUESTIONS

- **What is being required of me that love would not naturally demand?**
- **Who regulates when tension appears?**
- **Does my presence restore peace — or merely prevent discomfort?**
- **Does this relationship make obedience to God lighter or heavier?**

Where obedience becomes heavier, an illegal knot is present. Anything that must be maintained through guilt, fear, or pressure is not held together by love, it is held together by force. That force may be subtle, but Heaven recognizes it. Some entanglement knots will fall apart quickly. Others require patience, clarity, and consistent standing. No illegal knot is permanent. Authority precedes freedom, and freedom is always lawful.

SIGNS OF ENTANGLEMENT

Well, dang — is that a pimple or a mosquito bite? Same symptom. Very different cause. Very different treatment. Pop a mosquito bite? You make it worse. Put anti-itch cream on a pimple? You don't solve the problem. If you treat entanglements like soul ties, then you will apply the wrong remedy, then wonder why nothing changes.

Drop the blame and get the right diagnosis. If you misdiagnose the issue, you'll misapply the cure — and then assume the cure doesn't work. Not everything that itches needs to be broken. Some things just need to be untangled.

The following are signs that you are in an entanglement or entangled:

Confusion replaces clarity -You don't know "what this is," and that bothers you.

Boundaries feel rude - Even when you owe them nothing.

Your spirit feels crowded - Like someone else is "in the room."

Mental rehearsals - You keep going over conversations in your head.

Atmospheric disturbance - You lose Peace around them.

Emotional imbalance - You feel too much or too little based on tiny interactions.

Guilt shows up for no reason - You don't want to disappoint them.

You feel pulled - Not led or guided--, **pulled.**

You feel responsible for their feelings - Even lightly.

You feel spiritually foggy when dealing with them – Light that you normally feel sort of dims.

You keep trying to "clean it up" - But it gets messier.

You don't want to disappoint them …but you're not actually in covenant with them.

    You know you're entangled when you feel confusion instead of clarity. You feel responsible for someone you don't even actually know. You rehearse conversations in your mind. They accuse your boundaries of being rude to them. They are intrusive. You feel emotional imbalance. Their presence shifts your atmosphere. You feel pushed or pulled — coerced, rather than led, or that your desires are respected. You feel guilty for pulling back, or fear that you should stay in the connection with them. Their opinion has unauthorized weight. You lose Peace but can't explain why.

Entanglements never feel Godly, because they are not. They feel intrusive or **sticky.**

Divine covenants, conversely, produce life, allows movement, strengthens obedience to God. Entanglement restricts movement, competes with obedience, requires appeasement to maintain peace.

Covenant multiplies strength. Entanglement consumes it.

Entanglements exist because something is being sought that cannot be lawfully obtained. This is a conflict in authority. Entanglements are put in place as a *workaround* to God's way. Entanglements are knots and they are illegal.

What love gives freely, entanglement must extract. Resistance appears because authority is being contested. Scripture does not describe this conflict as negotiation. *"We wrestle not against flesh and blood..."* (Ephesians 6); but we do wrestle. Wrestling implies opposing objectives. One side wrestles to bind. The other wrestles to remain free. The aggressor seeks restriction. The Believer is instructed to stand.

Standing is an act of authority.

Illegal knots often appear in marriages, dysfunctional families and ministries, fake friendships, and in ungoverned workplaces. God joins bodies in covenant, not consciences in captivity. People often excuse entanglement by saying, *We're married. We're family. We're close.*

Entanglements may look like guilt or autonomy. They could present as pressure to regulate another adult's emotions. They may show up as a loss of Peace when you are not doing what the other person wants. They could look like urgency without wrongdoing. Or they could feel like obligation without agreement. These are not signs of love deepening; they are signs of authority being overreached.

Entanglements are not formed in one moment. They are formed through repeated, unchallenged concessions. Every time someone abandons Peace to relieve pressure, rushes to prevent another's discomfort, complies without agreement, accepts guilt without wrongdoing, a knot tightens, not dramatically, but incrementally.

Authority is not stolen; it is yielded.

An entangler wants you to leave your authority and yield it to them. Entanglements are illegal and they are for the purpose of control.

WHAT MAKES A KNOT ILLEGAL

An illegal knot is not defined by pain alone, although there may be emotional duress and pressure. Entanglements are defined by **authority**. A knot is illegal when it restricts something God never authorized to be bound, such a movement, conscience, obedience, rest, or personal governance. The presence of affection, history, covenant language, or good intentions does **not** legitimize a restriction God did not assign.

Illegality is not about *how it feels*. It is about *who has jurisdiction*.

Most illegal knots are not formed by villains; some people have good intentions, but it doesn't make what they are doing right. These knots are formed by anxiety, fear of loss, insecurity, unmet needs, or even misapplied Scripture.

Likewise, most people who become entangled are not weak. They are often responsible, empathetic, peace-oriented, and spiritually serious. Illegal knots frequently form involving good people, which is why they can persist unnoticed.

An illegal knot becomes something that does not naturally flow from love, covenant, or agreement. As a test, answer this question carefully, *What is being taken that would not freely be given without pressure?*

If pressure is required, if there is guilt, urgency, fear, withdrawal, or obligation, then authority and jurisdiction has been exceeded.

Love does not need leverage. Authority does not need coercion.

Now do the yoke test. Jesus provides the clearest jurisdictional standard *"My yoke is easy, and My burden is light."* (Matthew 11). A yoke that tightens under rest, punishes autonomy, produces anxiety for obedience, or requires appeasement to maintain peace is not Christ's yoke, regardless of who placed it. God's yoke governs direction, not breathing.

HOW DID THIS HAPPEN?

Was there something in me that allowed this?" Allowing an illegal knot does not mean you *wanted* it. It usually means you valued Peace, you feared conflict, you misunderstood duty, you confused patience with permission, or you believed love required endurance. Many illegal knots are tolerated because they appear *virtuous* at first.

But tolerance is not authorization.

Some entanglements are unknowingly in place and therefore allowed even though a person may ignore early discomfort, override internal warnings, explain away pressure, spiritualize obligation, call appeasement love, or call endurance submission. None of these make the knot legal. They simply make it uncontested. Authority that is not exercised does not disappear; it is simply unused.

Love Bombing is an early entanglement signal. Yes, you are *all that*, and maybe someone would be just wild over you, but nobody is **ALL THAT,** so be realistic.

Love bombing is often an early attempt to accelerate attachment before authority, trust, or discernment are established.

That places it squarely in pre-entanglement behavior. Love bombing signals an entanglement attempt. It's like after a storm your surge protector is blown. There's a reason for that: too much electricity too fast. Pre-entanglements try to create a knot with very early access before there has been enough movement to notice it forming. Love bombing is often an early attempt to form attachment before authority and discernment are in place. It does not always succeed, but when unexamined, it can become the first strand of an illegal knot.

Healthy affection remains steady if you slow down, respect boundaries, do not require immediate reciprocity, respect and independent movement. Love bombing intensifies when you hesitate, escalates when you set boundaries, withdraws when you pause, seeks reassurance through proximity. For example, the healthy-minded one welcomes time; the anxious or manipulating one fears it.

Anything that requires speed to secure closeness is not trusting love, it is anxious attachment seeking control. Love that must rush to bind is already afraid of losing access.

One of the clearest signs of an illegal knot is you felt a check within you, but you learned to dismiss it. There was a subtle internal pause that said, *"Something about this costs more than it should."* Ignoring conscience is the first problem; it creates **vulnerability**. What you are calling conscience may be you ignoring or quenching the Holy Spirit and that is against what God said.

Scripture does not command Believers to carry another adult's emotional regulation, surrender conscience to preserve Peace, or abandon obedience to maintain harmony. The Bible says that the married person considers how to please a spouse, but the unmarried is concerned with pleasing God. (1 Corinthians 7). This is not hierarchy; it is order. Pleasing a spouse is relational; it is not court jestering or being a standup comic, unless of course, you are a stand-up comic. Obeying God is governmental. The former never overrides the latter.

Illegal knots persist when authority was left unguarded. When we are distracted, sometimes that can happen. When love is sincere, intentions are good, we feel that we are in a very safe place or we don't want to rock the boat because conflict would feel *unspiritual*.

Of course, conflict didn't affect Jesus like that, but too many Christians think that being a Christian means being nice. Just nice.

Scripture does not call believers to be *unboundaried, it says we should* stand and *"Stand therefore..."* (Ephesians 6). Standing is not aggression. It is refusal to yield what should not be granted or abandoned.

If an illegal knot forms, that does not mean you failed. It means you tolerated something God never required.

Tolerance can be unlearned.

Authority can be reclaimed.

Knots can be loosened.

Entanglements can be completely untangled, unbraided.

DISCERNMENT CHECKPOINT

Is This a Soul Tie, an Entanglement, or a Siege?

Before you attempt to untie anything, you must identify what kind of restraint you are dealing with. Not every restriction is relational. Not every pressure is personal. Not every delay is demonic. Misidentifying the conflict leads to misapplied solutions.

1. A **Soul Tie** is a *bond of affection, loyalty, or identity* formed through intimacy, shared history, covenant, or trauma.

Key markers are emotional attachment, longing or grief, difficulty letting go, and memory-driven pull. It affects the *heart*. Primary work required: Healing, closure, truth, time, and sometimes mourning. Unhealed, a soul tie pulls you backward.

2. An **Entanglement** is an illegal knot where access, control, or regulation is **taken without authority**. Key markers are guilt without wrongdoing, pressure to remain small, restriction of movement. If you try to return to our own autonomy, you may feel anxious. In an entanglement, peace restored only through compliance with what the other person wants or wants you to do.

Entanglements affect *Authority and movement*. Primary work required: Discernment, standing, boundary restoration, withdrawal of consent. An entanglement holds a person in one place.

3. A **Siege** is external opposition aimed at exhaustion, isolation, or surrender, not attachment. Key markers are pressure from outside the relationship, scarcity, delay, resistance without intimacy, attacks on resources, time, or morale, no emotional bond with the source. It affects *endurance and faith*. Primary work required is perseverance, spiritual authority, strategy, and patience. A siege pushes from the outside.

You don't warfare-pray your way out of an entanglement. You don't boundary-set your way out of a siege. You don't stand firm against a soul tie.

Right diagnosis preserves energy, clarity, and obedience. You cannot untie what must be healed, and you cannot heal what must be resisted.

A would-be entanglement is an attempted linkage that: has not been agreed to, has not been purchased, has not been covenanted, has not been clarified, and is knowingly against the victim's will, yet is treated *as if it already exists*.

Assumed proximity is not consent. common forms of would-be entanglements:

1. **Positional Entanglement** - Someone behaves as if they hold authority they were never granted.

2. **Brand / Identity Entanglement** - Names, images, goodwill, or reputation are blended without agreement.

3. **Labor Entanglement** - Work is requested or expected without clear compensation or scope.

4. **Visibility Entanglement** - Public-facing actions (videos, announcements, representations) are used to imply partnership.

5. **Asset Entanglement** - Space, equipment, or infrastructure is treated as shared when it is not.

6. **Relational Proxy Entanglement** - Spouses, family, or associates are inserted to perform labor or create obligation.

Would-Be Entanglements Advance because they :move faster than paperwork. They rely on silence, politeness, or delay. They exploit ambiguity. They benefit from your professionalism. They collapse boundaries by acting *"as if"*. Entanglements rarely announce themselves; they presume.

Fend off entanglements and would-be entanglements preventatively.

1. **Control forward-facing assets**
   (media, messaging, branding, digital presence)

2. **Decline premature visibility**
   ("I'm not available" is sufficient)

3. **Separate assets early**
   Quiet removal prevents later disputes.

4. **Avoid explanatory language**
   Explanations invite negotiation.

5. **Document facts, not feelings**
   Facts keep exits clean.

6. **Honor discomfort without dramatizing it**
   Discomfort is data.

The governing principle is that "not every approach is an assignment. Not every proximity is permission. Not every invitation is safe to accept." Discernment is recognizing what you are being invited *into* before you step.

Look well to your flocks, if what you own is not looked over then anything could be happening. We are spirits we need spiritual covering and that is foremost by us, spiritual awareness. Jesus said, "I felt virtue flow out of Me." Virtue is spiritual so that touch was not just physical it was spiritual with spiritual intent. That's deep discernment. Pray for that.

KNOTS & ENERGY

Knot formation takes strategy and it consumes energy. Knots create strain under tension, and their presence soaks up energy. They require intentional effort to undo. These knots are not accidentally made. What God joins bears weight with ease. What man knots tightens under pressure. If maintaining a relationship requires more energy than pursuing obedience, a knot has formed. Peace that requires constant effort is not Peace; it is managed tension.

Life flows. But knots resist flow. Whatever resists life must eventually be untied.

An *illegal knot* means someone tied what they had no right to tie. That means an illegal person or persons, or someone that you allowed who is acting illegally, whether they realize it or not (but most often they do). Someone restricted what they were not authorized to restrict. something voluntary was converted into something compulsory. That is the essence of entanglement.

If it's illegal, it can be undone.

Entanglements are illegal knots. They are formed when access is taken without authority, when closeness is enforced rather than chosen, and when what should flow freely is extracted through pressure.

ENTANGLEMENT VERSUS HEALTHY INTERDEPENDENCE

If your person is forever wanting to know *where are you?* or *where have you been?* you might have an entanglement problem. If distance, or your absence creates guilt. Autonomy feels like betrayal. One person manages the other's emotional state. Peace depends on proximity. *Does time apart require justification? Does coming home, even though they may ignore you the whole time you both are home--, but does it restore emotional order? Does the relationship regulate through control?* Then you have an entanglement problem.

In healthy interdependence, distance is neutral, autonomy is respected; each person self-regulates. Togetherness is chosen, not demanded. Time apart does not damage the bond. Reunion is joyful, not corrective. The relationship regulates *through trust*.

Does my presence restore peace, or simply prevent discomfort? If your presence is needed to *prevent* someone else's unease, you are drifting toward entanglement. If your presence is welcomed but not required for emotional stability, that's interdependence.

When closeness is required to regulate another adult's emotions, the relationship has shifted from partnership into containment.

In asymmetrical entanglement the controlling one is doing the tugging and the other is the 'workhorse.' Entanglement *does* often have a "tugging side" and a "working side." This means that the entanglement is structured to benefit one person and not the other. In many entanglements, there is one party who initiates pressure. Then, the other party absorbs, adjusts, compensates, and carries. That does not always mean overt domination, conscious scheming, cruelty. But it *does* mean unequal emotional labor and regulation.

In a healthy partnership/relationship/marriage, both walk at agreed pace. Direction is discussed. Strength is shared. In an entanglement one side applies tension, The other side supplies movement. The "tugging" side signals discomfort through tone, withdrawal, expectation, guilt, silence, urgency. They may frame needs as closeness, togetherness, priority, or concern. They often believe *their anxiety is proof of love.*

The "workhorse" side adjusts speed, plans, desires. Carries the burden of harmony. They learn to anticipate pressure before it's applied. They make moves, maybe all the moves to prevent relational friction. The defining feature is which one self-regulates and who is regulated by the other.

The "tugging" side is not always stronger. Often they are more anxious and more threatened by autonomy. Many times, they are less able to tolerate separateness. The workhorse is often more stable, more capable, more conscientious, more peace-oriented.

Entanglement exploits strength, not weakness. Direction is controlled through tension. The workhorse moves *to relieve pressure*. The tugging side rarely notices the effort but expects this is normal. They think that this is how it should be. (My partner should anticipate my needs and give me what I desire, deserve, and want.)

One regulates. One compensates.

In an entanglement, one partner applies tension to maintain closeness, while the other supplies movement to preserve peace.

Ask yourself this: *When tension appears, who changes?* If one consistently adapts while the other remains static that is an entanglement. If both adjust through conversation, that's a proper partnership. In a healthy bond no one needs a bridle. No one is *worked.* No one is steered through guilt. Direction is self-chosen. Pace is mutual. Rest is permitted.

Biblically, it is normal to seek to please one's spouse, but that doesn't mean over compensating, shrinking. Nor does it mean loss of self-governance.

My yoke is easy, and My burden is light.

A yoke implies shared direction and shared load. It never implies strangulation, jerking, or fear-based control. If a yoke tightens when you pause, or pulls when you breathe, it is no longer Christ's yoke, regardless of who is holding the reins.

Pleasing your spouse is voluntary. Entanglement is compulsory. Scriptural pleasing flows from love, remains choice-driven, does not punish rest, or absence. Neither does it require appeasement.

Entangled pleasing is driven by anxiety, is enforced by guilt, collapses autonomy, and restores Peace only through compliance.

Many Believers confuse consideration with containment, submission with self-erasure, unity with fusion. But Scripture never commands a spouse to become the regulator of another's emotions, the keeper of another's peace, nor the stabilizer of another's insecurity. Those roles belong to God.

The sister of a fellow I was seeing said, "I don't know what you are doing to make my brother so happy but keep it up."

Instantly I responded, "I'm not doing anything to make or keep him happy. He is in charge of his own emotions and emotional well-being." That didn't go over too well, his family thought I was harsh because as I'd find out later, he had them all entangled and even as an adult who lived in his own house he still ran the family of origin with his *moods*.

It was the truth anyway and I was not going to be entangled in such. That is between that man and God.

Pleasing a spouse is an expression of love; carrying a spouse's emotional burden is a substitution for God. That is the line entanglement crosses.

The Yoke Test: *Does this relationship make obedience to God lighter — or heavier?* If pleasing your spouse competes with Peace, the yoke is wrong. If pleasing your spouse coexists with freedom, the yoke is aligned. God's yoke never requires rushing out of joy, guilt for rest, anxiety for distance, fear of displeasing man.

A spouse may be *pleased*; God must be *obeyed*. No human yoke is authorized to override conscience, calling, rest, or God's governance of the soul.

This touches on authority again, where the entanglement wants something out of the entangled that they would not normally or naturally give. Entanglement seeks to extract what it cannot lawfully receive.

This is like wrestling (Ephesians 6). The aggressor may be wrestling to get a person INTO a knot, while the Believer is wrestling to NOT be tied or to get out of a knot.

NOT AUTHORIZED

Entanglement wants what it is not authorized to have. In a healthy relationship, what flows between two people is voluntary, whether it is affection, presence, attention, service, or consideration. In an entanglement, one party seeks more than the relationship naturally yields, such as emotional regulation, identity reassurance, constant availability, surrender of autonomy, prioritization over God, conscience, or calling.

That extra demand requires pressure, not love. That's where authority is being contested.

The aggressor wrestles to tie, we will call that entanglement wrestling. The Believer wrestles to stand or be free. That is the kind of wrestling that the Good Book speaks of; that is spiritual wrestling. Those are two different kinds of wrestling with two opposing objectives.

A. Entanglement Wrestling (To Bind). The entangling force is trying to reduce movement limit range, fix position, secure control. Like hogtying, the goal is not immediate harm — it is restricted agency.

Once tied, resistance weakens, direction is imposed, energy is spent just maintaining balance. That is why entanglement feels *draining*, not dramatic.

I saw a photo online of someone that I know very well. Beside him was a lovely young woman. It looked as if they were going to or had been to a fancy event. They were dressed to the nines. They were both smiling as if everything was okay, but what struck me is that the woman wasn't standing straight. It was not as though anything physically was wrong with her; she seemed healthy, but she was not standing plumb or fully vertical. It appeared to me at that moment is this woman is doing all she can to even stand up. I felt in my spirit, she looks drained, like he is draining the life out of her. Even with all the trappings, it was so close to a hostage, proof of life image that it was unsettling.

This guy is a known love bomber; he is over the top and relentless. This must be his next victim is what I thought to myself. I do not speculate when I say, she is in an entanglement, big time. I am not speculating because I know this man; and I know him from years ago--, like that.

People always say, if you want to know what kind of man a man is, then look at his wife. Is she okay???

B. Spiritual Wrestling is to remain untied. Paul's instruction is not win, overpower, or dominate, but it is "*Stand. Which* means to maintain your own autonomy and authority. It could mean refusing false guilt, resisting unlawful claims, maintaining God-given authority, not surrendering ground. Stand your ground. This *wrestling* is defensive, not aggressive. You are not trying to bind the other person. You are trying to stay free.

This is ongoing, and our daily choices and decisions matter. We must maintain self-governance because authority is honored, not enforced.

Every time you rush to relieve someone else's anxiety, surrender peace to avoid discomfort, comply without agreement, or abandon joy to restore "order" or keep the peace, you are loosening your own stance. Maybe it's not all at once, but knot by knot.

Entanglement does not happen in one move. It happens through repeated concessions. Entanglement does *not* mean the other person has authority over you, it means you are being pressured to yield authority that you actually possess. That's why the struggle exists. If they already had it, there would be no wrestling.

Entanglement is a struggle over authority: one side seeks access it was never granted; the other must decide whether to stand or surrender. What love gives freely, entanglement must extract.

Discernment Test: Ask yourself: *What is being requested that does not flow naturally from love, agreement, or covenant?*

That access demand is where wrestling begins, pressure increases, guilt is introduced. And that is exactly why and where authority must be exercised.

God's yoke does not require wrestling to breathe. If you are fighting not to be tied, you are not resisting love, you are defending governance. You are saying they are unauthorized.

Knots limit movement, consume energy, create strain under tension, require intentional effort to undo. Knots are *made*. They are created on purpose and are not accidental. Entanglements don't just *happen*. Anything that must be maintained through guilt, fear, or pressure is not held together by love; it is held together by force.

ILLEGAL KNOTS & HUMAN RELATIONSHIPS
Cinema Magic

This chapter is simply because I don't want anyone to fall for this. Have you ever noticed in movie plots they compress "love" into days or weeks? That is not done because that is how love or relationships start or work, it is because that's easy for cinema. Movies are full of entanglement triggers instead. Two people meet during crisis, travel, fall into danger together, suffer loss, or transition and magically they *fall in love*. Those conditions lower boundaries and heighten emotional openness. That creates *false intimacy* quickly; in real life that is entanglement, not love.

A couple meet, they are thrown together, in some way, romantic, antagonistic or some other way, for a short time period, like throwing laundry in a dryer. After a few tumbles the cycle is done and they are in love. Through *projection*, each person fills in the blanks with hope, fantasy, unmet needs, and that feeling of "this feels different." They're not loving the person — they're loving who they imagine the person to be. That's not love. That's identity borrowing.

Narrative pressure in movies (and real life) goes something like this: *We met at the perfect time. It feels meant to be. Everything lined up.* That language creates meaning inflation, which binds people prematurely. That's another entanglement mechanism.

Physiology plays a big part in this in real life, and it is displayed on the movie screen. Chemicals such as dopamine (reward), oxytocin (bonding), and adrenaline (shared intensity) are involved. Those are powerful, but temporary.

Love is what remains after those settle.

Fast "love" often equals accelerated access, unearned emotional authority, assumed future, premature loyalty. In other words, this really is connection without order, connection without governance.

That's an entanglement, not a bond.

Ask, *Has this relationship made me more grounded, or more fused?* Real Love increases clarity, agency, patience, and discernment. Entanglements are like a timeshare pitch; they increase, urgency, fear of loss, identity blending, pressure to decide *now*.

Don't be deceived, this is not how it works in real life. Movies glorify the second and call it love.

It *feels* convincing because entanglements borrow the language of love, destiny, soulmates.

- I've never felt this way.
- When you know, you know.

Movies compress love into days because entanglements are faster than covenants, and more cinematic. Real love is quieter, harder to film, but it is far more durable.

Please don't think that if you just go to the cabin with him that he will propose, just like in the movies. Nope; that's not how it works. Movies have trained people (especially the immature, the hopeful, or the lonely) to confuse proximity + intensity with commitment.

Movies collapse time for the sake of the movie. Real life does not. Films teach us that a weekend away, a cabin trip, a shared crisis, a long conversation by a fire …can produce love, clarity, and a proposal. No. That is not love. That is accelerated emotional access.

Accelerated access does not create covenant; it creates entanglement. *If I just go away with him for a weekend, he'll know. If we're alone long enough, something will happen. If we share something intense, it will seal the bond.*

Nope. What it often seals instead is misplaced hope, assumed meaning, unequal expectation, emotional leverage. Those are the ingredients of entanglement, not love.

Time reveals character. Intensity only reveals chemistry. Love does not need a compressed timeline to prove itself.

If someone needs isolation, pressure, urgency a getaway, or a "special moment" to decide whether they want you...they are not choosing *you,* they are choosing the **experience**. Experiences fade. Entanglements unravel, but real love remains steady.

Please don't set yourself up with false hope and wishful or fantasy thinking.

Movie love timelines are not real. Two-day destiny bonds are not real; they are **scripts,** and scripts are powerful until someone calmly says, That's a movie. This is real life. Lust is real life and there can be major chemistry between two people. Know this: Lust lasts about 2 years, then either of you will be looking at the other wondering, *"What was I thinking?"*

Culture hands us scripts the way children are handed costumes. They look convincing until someone tells the truth: Storm Troopers are not real, and neither is two-day love. Some things feel real because we've seen them often. That doesn't make them true.

Dear Reader: understand this so you won't be disappointed or tricked.

RECOGNIZING YOU'RE ENTANGLED

Most people do not recognize an entanglement while they are in it. *Why?* Because entanglements are **silent at first**. They do not announce themselves. They do not feel like danger. They do not feel like they are in bondage or that they are under attack. There is an emotional charge to entanglements. There is an anointing that made it happen in the first place. That anointing or charge is designed to make the one that is roped in feel excited, distracted, it's okay, or it's going to be okay.

Entanglements feel like concern; Oh they really care about me. They feel like curiosity, connection, or obligation, They may feel like, God is highlighting this person. Or, *Wow, they really care about me so much.* Or, *I don't know why I care so much.* And deeper than that, *I feel spiritually connected to them somehow. This must really mean something.*

It's spiritual alright, but God does not sponsor entanglements.

The enemy does not begin entanglements with chaos; he begins them with care, concern and meaning. *Which route are you taking home? Call me as soon as you get there.* Meaningfulness is the camouflage of entanglement.

This chapter reveals the undeniable signs that a knot has formed.

We have visited this list in a condensed form at the start of this book, but now there will be some examples that may bring more clarification to each Sign of Entanglement.

SIGN #1 — CONFUSION REPLACES CLARITY. *If they cost you clarity, they cannot be from God.* The very first sign of entanglement is mental or spiritual confusion.

Examples:

- You can't tell what the relationship *is*.
- You can't describe the connection, and many times they **won't** describe it.
- You're unsure what you "owe" them.
- You feel pulled but don't know why.
- Your peace shifts around them.
- Your thoughts feel noisy.

Confusion is not a symptom; it is a **diagnosis.**

When a connection is God-ordained, clarity comes quickly. Discernment lands fast. Peace arrives early. Entanglements create fog, uncertainty, questions, internal noise, and lack of peace. If the connection cannot be explained, defined, or categorized, you are tangled.

SIGN #2 — YOUR EMOTIONS FEEL PULLED, NOT LED. The Holy Spirit leads. Whereas entanglements pull. This is the emotional hijack. You feel drawn, tugged, unsettled, emotionally activated, overly sensitive to them, guilty when you distance, strangely connected or hooked on them.

Your emotions do not feel like your own. You're not choosing your feelings; feelings are choosing you. When someone has emotional influence without emotional legitimacy, you are entangled.

SIGN #3 — YOU FEEL RESPONSIBLE FOR THEIR FEELINGS. Not their welfare. Not their well-being. Their **feelings**.

You begin to ask:

- "Are they upset with me?"
- "Did I let them down?"
- "Did I hurt their feelings?"
- "Should I reach out?"
- "Should I fix it?"

- "Did I do something wrong?" And the worst possible summation of this list: *"They don't like me anymore."*

Even when you did nothing. They are not your assignment. They are not your responsibility. You owe them nothing. They are not your covenant. They are not your partner. They are not your leader. They are not in your inner court. False responsibility is a red flag of entanglement. You are not responsible for another grown person's feelings and anyone who tries to make you believe that is trying to use Jedi mind tricks on you to entangle you.

False responsibility is spiritual vulnerability disguised as compassion.

This is not a call to become cold, distant, or emotionally unavailable. Scripture never asks us to lack natural affection or to withdraw kindness from others. We are meant to be compassionate, considerate, and willing to repair when we have caused harm.

You are called to love people, not to live inside their emotions. You can be gentle, caring, and attentive without taking responsibility for another adult's inner world. Empathy allows connection without surrendering jurisdiction. Healthy affection does not require you to carry what God assigned them to manage.

Warmth is not the same as emotional obligation.

SIGN #4 — YOU REHEARSE CONVERSATIONS IN YOUR MIND is one of the strongest signs. You replay what they said, how you responded, what you should've said, how they might react, what the next conversation will be, how to explain your boundaries, how to fix the vibe. You are forever making Peace, trying to keep the Peace (if it really exists), you may be walking on eggshells. It's a mess and a lot of work for you. Most of it is impossible work because after the entanglement begins or the knot is fully formed, who is to say the threads won't tighten?

This is mental captivity. This is cognitive entanglement, a knot in the mind. You are not thinking *about them; y*ou are thinking *around them.* Orbiting them. They have become a mental gravity point; if this is not idolatry, it is very close to it. That is NOT connection. That is entanglement.

SIGN #5 — YOUR PEACE DISAPPEARS IN THEIR PRESENCE. This one is surgical. You do not need discernment to detect entanglement; you need PEACE.

Ask yourself these questions: *Do I feel lighter or heavier after interacting with them? Does my peace rise or fall? Does my spirit rest or react? Does my mind quiet or race? Does my atmosphere settle or shift?*

Peace is your spiritual gauge. Peace is your internal compass. Peace is the witness of the Holy Spirit. When Peace leaves, entanglement enters.

SIGN #6 — YOU BEGIN TO MINIMIZE YOURSELF. You shrink. Even subtly. You become quieter, more cautious, less confident, more self-conscious, more aware of how you appear, less anchored in your identity. You begin to think about YOU through THEM. This is **identity drift.**

It means the cord of identity distortion is active. You are no longer standing fully in your own spirit; your identity has been tied.

SIGN #7 — YOUR DISCERNMENT TURNS "OFF" WHERE THEY ARE CONCERNED. With everyone else, you're clear. With them, you're foggy. Things you would easily detect in others… you overlook in them. Warnings you would normally heed… you excuse.

Red flags you would normally run from… you reinterpret. This is not love. This is not familiarity. This is not intuition. This is spiritual interference. Entanglements interfere with discernment by dulling your internal alarms, clouding your prophetic senses, muting your intuition, overriding your normal judgment. If your discernment works everywhere except with *one person* — you are entangled.

SIGN #8 — YOU FEEL THEIR EMOTIONS IN YOUR BODY. Emotional transfer creates heaviness, anxiety, restlessness, sadness, pressure, guilt, longing, and unease. It's not just because *you* feel these things, but because they do. You are absorbing emotional energy. So, when they say, *"You feel me?"* You can really say you do, because you do. This is not discernment, this is entanglement.

Think about how wrong and weird this is: that person should be feeling their own *feels*, why are you tied to their emotions like an emotional support beast to help them feel their own emotions?

Discernment sees. Entanglement absorbs. Discernment perceives. Entanglement carries. Discernment identifies. Entanglement internalizes. If your emotions react to their emotional state, you are not simply connected; you are **knotted.**

A person once thought I was entangled emotionally or some other way with them. Without even having a fight, I was talking to them, but they turned their back on me, refusing to answer. I was going about my usual routine, and they are staring at a wall.

Whatever? I was married to that before, so it didn't work on me.

I wondered what was wrong with them and went on with whatever I was doing. They did not understand why this didn't work. It didn't work on me because I was not entangled with them. Their behavior or misbehavior was their problem and had nothing to do with me.

It would not be this way for anyone who is entangled. That person could be easily manipulated by the manipulator's actions, behaviors or feelings.

9. YOU FEEL GUILTY FOR WANTING DISTANCE. Guilt is the emotional leash of entanglement. For example:

You pull back because you feel bad. You set boundaries but then you feel like you're being too mean. You stop responding quickly, but then you feel wrong. And then you worry, what if they get mad at me?

You say, *No,* but then you feel selfish.

You protect your Peace, but you feel disloyal. This is the cord of expectation tightening. They have assumed a role, and your spirit is reacting to that assumption.

Guilt is not the Holy Spirit, nor is it Love. Guilt is not covenant. Guilt is a symptom of entanglement.

You're at the mall. No agreement was violated. No emergency exists. But you feel an internal pull to hurry, shorten your time, or abandon what you were doing because your spouse "wants you home." That is not time management; That is internalized pressure.

What makes this an entanglement signal, rather than love? Well ---, the guilt is not logical. Yet you feel unease, tension, or urgency. That points to relational enmeshment, not conscience.

The pressure exists without a spoken demand. There is no text, no call, no rule. But your *body* reacts anyway. That means the control has moved inside you. This is how entanglement matures: *External expectation becomes internal self-correction.*

Your own autonomy triggers anxiety. You are not doing anything wrong. You are simply not being immediately available, like waiting to return a phone call or a text. But, that creates discomfort in you.

Healthy attachment tolerates absence. Entanglement interprets absence as disloyalty.

The entangled will rush to restore "relational equilibrium." You don't *want* to leave, you just want the feeling to stop. So, you cut the trip short, speed up unnecessarily, Abandon enjoyment. This is appeasement behavior.

This is not honoring your spouse. It is not considering your family; it is not being thoughtful. Those things involve choice. This is different; this is pressure without agreement. It is guilt without cause. It is programmed obedience without instruction. This is control, and that's the line where entanglement begins.

Entanglement says, *"My comfort depends on your proximity."* That creates low-grade surveillance (even when unspoken). It could be real emotional dependency, or the other person could be faking you out for control. It could start with a subtle fear of independence, but over time, the person being entangled learns that *Peace exists only when I am where I'm expected to be, doing what I am expected to be doing.*

That is not covenant. That is containment.

A healthy marriage looks like this instead: Presence is chosen, not coerced. Distance is neutral, not threatening. Time apart does not require justification. Enjoyment does not require repayment. You return home because you *want to*—not because guilt chased you back.

A simple litmus test: *If I stayed another 30 minutes, would something actually be wrong—or would someone just be uncomfortable?*

If the answer is *discomfort without harm*, you are dealing with entanglement pressure, not marital duty. When autonomy produces guilt in the absence of wrongdoing, the relationship has crossed from attachment into entanglement.

So, if the mall-spouse doesn't come home to 'please' the home spouse's wishes does this mean that the manipulation didn't work, or the entanglement is not as deep (knotted/tied) as the home spouse desires? Answer: It usually means the entanglement didn't fully take, *not* that there was no attempt.

When the mall-spouse does *not* rush home to soothe the other's unspoken wishes, one of three things is happening (sometimes more than one):

1. The manipulation didn't internalize. The *signal* may have been sent (sighs, tone, past reactions, expectations), but it did not migrate inside the other person's conscience.

Entanglement only works when e*xternal pressure becomes internal self-policing.* If, however, the mall-spouse can say (even quietly), "I'm not doing anything wrong," and continue shopping, the knot didn't tighten.

2. The bond is not as knotted as the home spouse prefers. This is uncomfortable but important. Some people want a tighter tether than the relationship actually has. They may desire faster responsiveness. Emotional priority over autonomy. Reassurance through proximity. If the other person does not comply automatically, it reveals that t*he dependency is asymmetrical.*

Not every attempt to bind succeeds.

3. There is differentiation present. This is the healthy explanation. Differentiation means: *I can care about you without dissolving myself, or managing your feelings for you.* The mall-spouse's nervous system stays regulated, without rushing.

That alone blocks entanglement from deepening. This does **not** automatically mean the home spouse is evil, calculating, or consciously manipulative. Often it means they are uncomfortable with separateness. They experience distance as threat. They soothe anxiety through closeness. Intent and impact are not the same thing.

This whole example is based on something that really happened to me. One Saturday, I drove to the next town over from where I lived to pick up something that I had ordered from a certain store. I was on the phone with my then-boyfriend who lived in another city other than the one I lived in and the one I was driving to. He called me just as I was picking up the item and wanted to know where I was. I told him and then said, *"It's a nice mall, I'm going to stay and shop a little."*

He said, *"Oh, no you're not, I want you to get in your car and go to your house right now."*

I had never heard him speak like that before and then I was like, *Who is this guy right now? Is he serious?* And my go to: *Has he ever **met** me?* I said, Okay to him, hung up the phone and kept shopping. It was a very nice afternoon.

Entanglement much? I'm not saying I've never been entangled, but not that day.

SIGN #10 — YOU CANNOT EXPLAIN WHY THEY STILL HAVE SPACE IN YOUR SPIRIT

This is the signature sign. You don't even LIKE them like that. You don't WANT anything from them. You don't DESIRE closeness. You don't SEE a future. You don't FEEL compatible. Yet, they still have space in your inner world. This is where people say, "I don't want them, but something still feels unfinished. I don't even miss them, but they're still in my mind. I don't feel connected…but there's something still there. This "something" is the knot. Once formed, knots always remain even after feelings die.

If your spirit is not at Peace, your connection is not pure. Purity produces peace. Clarity produces peace. Alignment produces peace.

Entanglement produces confusion, emotional noise, and spiritual interference. When Peace leaves discernment speaks. When clarity lifts, God is signaling interruption. When something feels "off" — it usually is. Your spirit knows before your mind understands. And recognizing the signs is the FIRST STEP toward unbraiding.

DECLARATION

Lord, I recognize every sign of entanglement.
My spirit is alert. My mind is clear.
My emotions are settled. My discernment is active.
Every knot is exposed. Nothing hidden will remain tied.
In the Name of Jesus. Amen.

ENTANGLEMENTS VS SOUL TIES

Many people believe they are soul tied when they are actually entangled. If they misdiagnose the problem, they will apply the wrong remedy. People default to "soul tie" language because it's familiar in church culture, it feels spiritually active, it offers a sense of agency or maybe it promises quick relief. However, entanglements don't dissolve through renunciation alone. You can pray sincerely and still remain structurally bound.

When separation of people is God-initiated in Scripture, it is often decisive, geographic, and irreversible, not tentative or partial. They're gone.

God saved you but you may not know it yet, so you mourn and lament. But when it's time for God to break up an entanglement, whether you prayed or whether it was by His Mercy, you need to be thankful.

When God separates people, families, or nations, He usually does at least one of the following: creates physical distance, establishes different lands, assigns different lines / inheritances, introduces time and distance so re-entanglement isn't easy. Then God removes constant access.

Abram and Lot agreed, "Separate yourself from me… if you go left, I will go right." Not, "Let's keep visiting" "Let's process our feelings" "Let's stay close but set boundaries". They took different territories. Why? Because proximity was breeding strife and confusion.

When you break up with someone you don't have to remain enemies, but you also don't have to stay friends. Let it go. Jacob and Esau. After reconciliation, they do not live together. They reconcile *relationally* but remain geographically separate. Why? Because Peace does not require proximity — and proximity might undo Peace.

Regarding Israel and Egypt. God doesn't just change Pharaoh's heart and let Israel stay nearby. He takes them out, leads them through the wilderness, places a sea between them, gives them a land with boundaries. Because lingering proximity could recreate bondage.

The Tower of Babel: God doesn't negotiate behavior. He confuses language, scatters people and spreads them across the Earth.

Exile. When separation is necessary, God uses time, distance, and loss of access. Distance breaks entanglement faster than explanation ever will. When people remain close, habits reassert themselves, roles re-form, pressure returns, memory overrides discernment. Distance allows clarity, re-formation of identity, restoration of internal authority, and new patterns to emerge.

God doesn't say, *Just feel differently.* Or, *Try harder.* Or, *Forgive again and stay.* Like regular parents, he doesn't say, *Tell your brother you're sorry and now y'all go play.* He doesn't say, *Hug and make up.* He often says, in effect, *Go somewhere else.* That's not avoidance; that's reordering. When God separates, He often puts distance where confusion once lived. God separates far enough that the old pattern cannot easily follow.

Separation in Scripture is rarely about rejection. It's about preservation. And yes — it's often *very far away.* Because partial separation leaves entanglements intact. When someone thinks, *I'm soul tied,* they try soul-tie-breaking prayers, emotional renunciation, verbal declarations, and forgiveness statements. Those may help bond-level pain. But if the real issue is access, authority, obligation, proximity, structure, or role confusion, the prayer doesn't fail, it's just aimed at the wrong layer and that's the result of mislabeling.

When entanglement is mislabeled as a soul tie, people feel defective (Why am I not free yet?). they repeat prayers without change. They assume spiritual weakness. They miss the need for practical disentangling. Shame replaces clarity.

You cannot pray your way out of a structure you are still participating in. Soul ties respond to repentance and release. Entanglements respond to withdrawal of access and reordering of authority.

IDENTITY ENTANGLEMENTS

Identity Entanglements is the stealth category. They form when someone ties themselves to your purpose. You let a person define your calling. You see yourself through their opinion. You adopt their version of your destiny. Identity entanglements distort self-awareness. Someone once compared me to a known intercessor/deliverance minister. I couldn't identify with what they saw. I'm me, God made me; He may give the same gifts but with different administrations.

Identity/Assignment Entanglements sneak in when Someone ties into your calling. Your purpose intertwines with someone who shouldn't be there. Ministry partnerships form too fast. You start seeing yourself through THEIR perspective. These distort Identity. Self-perception. Direction. Calling, directly and structurally. This is the same mechanism, just expressed in different costumes.

The shared root is unfinished individuation. Whether it's calling "Mom" for every decision, needing a pastor, prophet, psychic, chart, or outsourcing choices to horoscopes or signs, the core issue is not spirituality, it's developmental.

Individuation is the process by which a person becomes internally referenced, capable of choice, responsible for outcomes, able to tolerate uncertainty, willing to bear consequences. When individuation is incomplete, people look **outside themselves** for regulation.

Parental dependence maps to false prophetic dependence. External authority replaces internal authority - *Mom tells me what to do. Prophet tells me what to do. Psychic tells me what's coming.* Different voice. Same function. Anxiety drives consultation; the call to mom or even a psychic isn't about information, it's about relief.

If someone tells me what to do, I don't have to feel the weight of choosing. That's not guidance; that's anxiety management. Responsibility is displaced. If things go wrong I can say, *"Mom told me..." "The prophet said..." "My chart indicated..."* That protects the ego from regret, accountability, and self-trust failure. But it also prevents autonomy, growth and maturity. Attachment masquerades as Wisdom. What looks like closeness, spirituality, respect, and humility is often dependency, fear of autonomy, avoidance of adulthood, resistance to separation. That is the entanglement.

This becomes spiritualized so easily because spirituality provides language of authority, permission to obey, justification for dependence, moral cover for avoidance. It feels *safer* to say, "God told me through them" than to say, "I don't trust myself yet."

False prophetic systems thrive on unindividuated adults. Not necessarily evil people, but unfinished ones. Calling Mom and calling Miss Cleo are cousins. One is socially acceptable. The other is stigmatized. Functionally both regulate anxiety. Both delay self-trust. Both outsource discernment. Both keep the caller psychologically childlike. The difference is *aesthetic*, not structural.

This is only one of the reasons why spiritual entanglements are so dangerous. They freeze development, sanctify dependence, reward passivity, punish discernment, and keep people "seeking" instead of *becoming*. They block, grieve and quench the Holy Spirit. The Holy Spirit is the Spirit of Guidance who leads into all Truth, not Miss Cleo and not your mother.

Entanglements can last decades. A person may grow old without ever growing up.

When external voices replace internal authority, entanglement forms. False prophetic dependence often succeeds where individuation never finished. What some call spirituality is sometimes just uncompleted adulthood with religious language.

Healthy guidance strengthens discernment, reduces dependency, leads toward autonomy.

Unhealthy guidance must be consulted repeatedly, increases anxiety, and replaces self-governance. Whether the number dialed is Mom or a hotline, the entanglement is the same.

Now, look at this same entanglement pattern running in the opposite direction. The flip side: reverse dependence / enmeshment. In this version, the *parent* has not individuated from the child. So instead of the child looking to the parent for regulation, you get the parent looking to the child for regulation. The child becomes the confidant, the decision partner, the emotional stabilizer, the validator, or the "second self". This is not closeness; it's an entanglement that is also role confusion.

In real life, the child appears to hold influence, but not authority; they are made responsible without being empowered. This is not shared leadership; it is abdicated governance. The child is not given authority, but they are given weight to carry.

The parent cannot make decisions without the child. The child is consulted on adult matters. The parent's identity collapses without the child's presence. The child feels responsible but may not feel chosen. Separation feels like betrayal, not growth. Loyalty replaces freedom.

This particular bond doesn't loosen with time; it hardens. That's an entanglement.

This happens because often the parent lacked support themselves, was emotionally isolated, didn't complete individuation earlier, substituted the child for adult companionship, fused identity with caretaking. So, the **child** becomes *"the one who sees me"* Which feels like love, but functions like glue.

There was a set of twins who worked in the same workplace. They dressed alike every day; they wore the same clothes but worked different shifts. By the other employees there, they were perceived as one person. This is textbook enmeshment, not novelty. It's not evil or weird, it's just unfinished separation. It's a classic case of *mutual non-individuation*, and it is common in twins.

Twins have shared developmental timelines, mirrored identity formation, external reinforcement of sameness. delayed differentiation pressures, and social permission to remain fused. So, if individuation is not actively supported, twins can become psychologically interchangeable, identity-blended, role-shared, decision-fused, mutually regulating.

The reason this is important is because the child to parent entanglement discussed previously was seen in a set of twins and each of their children toward them. Whether it's the child clinging to the parent, the parent clinging to the child, or a twin clinging to their own twin, the problem is not closeness, it's lack of differentiation.

Healthy bonds allow independent thought, separate decision-making, tolerable distance, non-catastrophic disagreement. On the other hand, entangled bonds cannot tolerate separation.

This kind of enmeshment freezes growth, replaces conscience with proximity, substitutes attachment for discernment, creates loyalty conflict, and prevents adult authority from forming.

Spiritually, it shows up as difficulty hearing God independently, confusion between love and obligation, guilt when choosing differently, fear of autonomy, resistance to calling that requires separation. These are just knots formed early and never worked loose.

As said and seen, these entanglements are not just in romantic relationships or just in families. But after separation these types of questions may be heard: *Why can't I move without them? Why does their opinion feel binding? Why does separation feel wrong, not just sad?*

Entanglement occurs whenever identity depends on proximity. Love that cannot survive separation has crossed into fusion.

As said, this is common in twins, and it is entanglement, but it can absolutely be reversed.

MENTORSHIP ENTANGLEMENTS

Mentorship is not externalized authority. Healthy mentorship has a defined purpose and a built-in expiration. Its function is to transfer skill, model thinking, offer perspective, sharpen discernment, accelerate maturity. The ideal mentor aims to make themselves eventually unnecessary; that's when they know they've done their job. They don't replace your judgment; they train it. A 60-year-old can absolutely have mentors, *if* those mentors are: situational (new season, new domain), consultative, that is, giving advice, not directives, bounded with a clear scope, and non-identity-based (not "who I am").

Examples of healthy late-life mentorship: learning a new field, entering a new role, refining craft, navigating transition, gaining wisdom from someone further along in a specific lane. That's not dependence. That's lifelong learning.

It crosses into entanglement when the relationship does any of the following. Makes decisions *for* the person. Becomes necessary for emotional regulation. Is consulted for routine choices. Is elevated to moral or spiritual authority. Discourages independent discernment. Is framed as "covering," "fathering," or "alignment" rather than counsel. At that point, the mentor has become a proxy conscience. That's not growth, that's regression.

About people who call pastors "Daddy. Hey, that's your business; I'm not judging, but I'm saying, that's not for me. To me, it is a category violation. Spiritually and psychologically, that language signals, unresolved parental hunger, identity diffusion, desire for protection over accountability, longing for attachment rather than instruction, substitution of authority for intimacy. Here's the key problem: Pastors are not parents. When pastoral authority is framed in parental terms, it invites: infantilization of adults, obedience over discernment, loyalty over conscience, dependency over maturity, abuse of power (even unintentionally). It creeps me out.

So, what do you call it when that pastor starts to date someone in the congregation if he's the 'daddy'?

Something is out of order. Well, to me, anyway.

I will call anyone any of the fivefold ministry gifts placing that title, that office in front of their name, but I personally cannot call anyone in a church role anything different. Hey, that's me.

Some adults *want* lifelong authority figures. This is not about stupidity or weakness. It's about tolerance for adulthood. Adult autonomy requires bearing consequences, sitting with uncertainty making imperfect choices, owning outcomes, being wrong without collapse. Some people find that intolerable.

So, they seek a *voice* to follow, a covering to hide under, a father or mother figure. They feel that kind of system absolves them of choice. It feels safer. It feels spiritual, but it freezes development.

Biblical leadership equips, exhorts, teaches, corrects, releases. It does not replace conscience, demand emotional dependency, assume parental identity over adults, require loyalty to the person, or infantilize the flock. Paul didn't want sons who never grew up; he wanted people who could stand.

Ask yourself, *Does this relationship make me more capable of governing myself — or less?* If less, it's not mentorship, it's entanglement. If it makes me more capable, then it's healthy guidance.

Mentors are fine — even lifelong mentors, if they are bounded and non-substitutive. External authority becomes dangerous when it replaces internal authority. Pastors are not parents. Jesus is the Good Shepherd and He has a Father. He indicated that He and the Father are one, but not that He, Himself is the Father, or that the Father is the Shepherd. A pastor is a shepherd.

Pastors are not parents. Did David become a *parent* to any of the sheep in his fields? Did Jesus who describes Himself as one who sticks closer than a brother ever say He was any one's parent? Scripture never authorizes pastors to occupy the role of **Father**. A pastor is a **shepherd**. A shepherd tends, guides, guards, and feeds. A shepherd does **not** originate life, identity, or authority. That belongs to **God alone**.

Jesus is the Good Shepherd — *and* He has a Father. He is one with the Father, yet He is not the Father. Unity is not role confusion. Oneness is not replacement. Jesus shepherds under the Father's authority, not instead of it.

When pastors are treated—or allow themselves to function—as *parents*, several illegal knots form. Congregants transfer childlike dependency to a human leader. Conscience becomes outsourced. Obedience to God is filtered through a person. Separation feels like betrayal rather than maturity. That is not discipleship; that is misplaced authority.

A shepherd guides those who already belong to God, protects without possessing, feeds without fusing, and leads without replacing God's voice. A shepherd who becomes a parent creates entanglement by role confusion.

Even when he uses father language, Paul says there are *many instructors* but **not many fathers**.

When a pastor becomes the emotional regulator, or is consulted before God, is feared to be disappointed, is treated as the source of safety, the ministry has shifted from shepherding to **substitution,** which always produces knots.

Pastors are shepherds, not parents. Any ministry that requires childlike dependence from adults has exceeded its authority. A shepherd leads toward God; a substitute parent competes with Him. Jesus shepherds under the Father. Pastors shepherd under Jesus. No one replaces God. When roles remain clear, life flows. When roles blur, entanglement forms.

Ask yourself: "Does this relationship make me more capable of governing myself — or less?" THAT'S GOOD. Ask that question anytime in any situation. Ask it of mentors, pastors, parents, friends, any kind of relationship. Ask it of spiritual systems and even institutions. The answer tells the truth without argument.

You think that was something? Wait until you get to the next section.

SPIRITUAL ENTANGLEMENTS

Spiritual entanglements can be formed in many ways, even by your own doing. Prayer partnerships formed too fast can create them. Prophetic dependence can create them. Spiritual coverings not ordained by God are the start of some of them. Spiritual exchanges with the wrong person are danger signs. Counsel from someone outside your *lane* is another danger sign. Shared secrets that bind instead of bless should be avoided. All of these situations distort your spiritual atmosphere and dull discernment.

Spiritual entanglements. This chapter is for your consideration. What is shared here is based on deliverance ground.

Wherever there was an entanglement in the Bible associated with a cord or a thread, that spoke of a spiritual *entanglement.* Fallen sons of God were accused of entangling with the daughters of men in Genesis 6 and that's how giants were created. Adam and Eve were not giants, so with their DNA, they didn't give birth to giants, so where did these giants come from? Babies come to Earth by means of a cord; an umbilical cord, but if the child who arrives on Earth is not the child God intended, then we must consider that an illegal entanglement was involved.

1. Tamar got Judah's cord.
2. Rahab and the red thread
3. The three-fold cord
4. John the Baptist being filled with the Holy Spirit from his mother's womb. And he was nurtured through an umbilical cord.
5. Holy Spirit overshadowing Mary to beget Jesus was the most direct spirit-to-human connection.

Is there some Hebraism about threads, cords, shoe latchets and the like? John the Baptist said that he was not worthy to undo Jesus' shoe. Abram wouldn't take anything from Abimelech, not even a shoelace, so no one could say that king made Abram rich. Threads were wrapped around twins in the Bible to indicate which one came out first. There's talk of a three-fold cord. And we recall that Tamar took Judah's cord as a pledge.

Threads, cords, sandals/shoe-latchets, and binding objects form a consistent symbolic language in Scripture. It's about authority, ownership, covenant, and jurisdiction. The core Hebraic idea is that in the Hebrew worldview, physical connectors (cords, threads, sandals, staffs, garments) often represent legal, spiritual, or relational claims. They answer questions like: *Who belongs to whom?, Who has authority?, Who owes whom?, Who is responsible?, Who is permitted to act?*

These are not decorative details. They are legal-symbolic markers. Shoes and shoe-latchets reference Authority & Right to Act. When John the Baptist says he is "not worthy to unloose the sandal strap" of Jesus, that's not humility theater. In ancient Israel, removing or handling someone's sandal was tied to legal authority, especially in matters of inheritance, redemption, and right of action (see Ruth 4).

So, John the Baptist is saying, in effect *"I am not authorized to take up even the lowest legal function in relation to Him."* John the Baptist has no jurisdiction.

2. Abram refusing thread or shoe-latchet (Genesis 14). Abram tells the king of Sodom he will take "not a thread, not a sandal strap." Why? Because taking even a token object could establish a claim. Abraham is saying, *"You will have zero grounds — material, symbolic, or legal — to claim you contributed to my increase."* He is implying that *there is absolutely no connection between you and I, not even a thread.*

This is anti-entanglement language. He refuses not just wealth, but even symbolic indebtedness.

3. Threads on Twins (Genesis 38: Perez & Zerah) The midwife ties a scarlet thread on Zerah's hand to mark priority and inheritance. The thread says, "This one has the claim. This one has precedence. But the narrative subverts it because Perez breaks through first.

The lesson is that external markers do not always determine true order, but they *attempt* to. Threads here are about claimed position.

4. Tamar Taking Judah's Cord, Seal, and Staff. Tamar takes Judah's seal (identity/authority), his cord (means of carrying authority). his staff (right to rule / lineage marker). She doesn't take money. She takes proof of jurisdiction. Later, when Judah is confronted, he recognizes. *"She is more righteous than I.* Because the objects testify. Cords here are not jewelry; they are evidence.

5. Three-Fold Cord (Ecclesiastes). "A three-fold cord is not easily broken" is not romantic. It's juridical. It means strength comes from rightly ordered binding, covenantal alignment, not emotional fusion. The warning is that two-fold cords can break; mis-tied cords can entangle. Not every cord is good. Illegal cords can be broken or separated. Only rightly ordered cords endure.

6. Threads versus Knots. In Hebrew thought, Threads = potential connection. Cords establish connection. Knots cause complication, resistance, or binding beyond intention. Knots imply time, tension, repeated crossing, unresolved strain.

This is exactly how entanglements form. Scripture consistently uses small binding objects to signal big relational realities. Authority, inheritance, obligation, and freedom are often encoded in who holds what.

Entanglement happens when symbols of connection outpace consent or calling.

> Their line has gone out through all the earth,
> and their words to the end of the world. (Psalm 19:4)

Line means a measured reach, an assigned boundary, and an ordered extension. Creation itself is said to have a line, that is, a governed transmission of truth and authority. Psalm 19 is saying, *Creation's testimony has jurisdiction everywhere.*

Line vs Cord vs Knot goes something like this: A thread indicates a potential connection. A cord signifies an established binding. A line is a *measured authority with a defined reach, and a k*not is the worst; it is a disordered binding, resistance, over-crossing. Entanglements happen when cords form without consent, lines are crossed, boundaries are ignored, knots replace Godly and decent order.

> On the day you were born your cord was not cut, nor were you washed with water to make you clean, nor were you rubbed with salt or wrapped in cloths. (Ezekiel 16:4)

The measuring line in the Prophets is about God assigning judges, or restoring territory. The lines have fallen for me in pleasant places, (Psalm 16:6). All of these are about alignment, because entanglement is not just "being connected." It is misaligned connection, unauthorized extension, blurred jurisdiction, violated measure. Entanglement happens when someone lives outside their line — or lets others live inside it.

FORGET ME KNOTS

Who or what has attached itself to you? Around you? And tried to tie you or worse, entangle you? we are still in spiritual entanglements and this section is one of the reasons I wrote this book. If you are not spiritually minded, or if you are not strong, this section may not be for you. It is written because of things that I know about, things I've seen, and even things that have happened to me.

These are the knots that you want any attacker or antagonist to forget. You want them to forget your name and lose your location.

There are things that happen in the spirit realm that we cannot see. However, we know that the enemy and his agents know the Bible as well or better than a lot of Christian Believers. They take what God says, and inspired to be written and they twist it to the negative whenever and however they can.

How they do this is not the scope of this book, else this book would be guilty of what it is describing; and it is not.

Entanglements happen in the spirit. What you see in the natural is a result of what has already happened in the spirit. If you are the type who senses, hears, sees, or feels spiritual things happen then you would have already prayed about any attempts to tie, knot, or entangle you. If you are an intercessor, for example and you definitely stay 'prayed up' no matter what, then you are spiritually covered and you have more than likely slammed the access door shut on anything concerning yourself and whomever you pray for in the spirit realm.

But whatever attempts delivery to your spiritual mailbox, if there is no blockage or protection, it will reach you.

Spiritual entanglements are, of course, invisible but on deliverance ground it is purported that these entanglements create "fruit" or some result that proves that there was entanglement. Firstly, they are a counterfeit of covenant but they are the dark kingdom's version of covenant. If you could think of being tied together to something that you never would agree to be tied to in real life you may get the idea. The goal of the dark kingdom is more than single fold, it is to stop you, block you, delay you, keep you from moving forward. Then, if you could be used in a way that you would never agree to, then the dark kingdom would try that too.

In some cultures what I'm writing about is a commonly known thing. In some cultures, it is not discussed at all.

THREE PRIMARY CATEGORIES OF ENTANGLEMENT

1. Willful Entanglements *(Chosen, invited, maintained)* These are entanglements a person **actively participates in**, even if unconsciously at first. **Characteristics** include: The person returns repeatedly. They ignore discomfort. They benefit in some way (relief, identity, protection, status). They resist separation when clarity comes.

Examples include: Ongoing prophetic dependence--, even false prophecy. Frequenting places where there is false prophecy, even if you say it's only for 'entertainment.' That includes psychics, astrologers, witch doctors, and the like. If you are involved in repeated or chronic mentor worship. Financial fusion for emotional security can create monetary entanglements. Staying in spiritually controlling environments despite awareness. It includes astral projection and other mystical-spiritual, occultic activities, no matter the reason.

Going into or trying to go into spiritual realms where you should not go or be is how these entanglements occur and how they are willful because you decided to go there and you decided to return there of your own accord. Now if you were induced to go that is one thing, but it you did not even try to resist, then that is on you, and in that case, *consent remains present.*

From this, freedom looks like Repentance, Boundary-setting, Responsibility, Tolerating the discomfort of separation. Important tone note. This is agency acknowledgment.

2. Forced Entanglements *(Imposed, unavoidable, survival-based).* These form when choice is absent or severely constrained. This could occur in childhood environments, family systems, power imbalances, economic dependence and also in religious authority structures. This is nearly unavoidable in trauma or coercion.

Examples

- Parent–child enmeshment
- Cultic church dynamics
- Financial dependence in abusive relationships
- Spiritual authority imposed during vulnerability

Consent is compromised or nonexistent.

From this, freedom looks like Recognition, Time, Support, Safety, Gradual differentiation. People in forced entanglements are not morally culpable for entering them but spiritually, they are in them and they must get out spiritually. *I didn't know*, or *It's not my fault* or *They made me* is usually not admissible for defense in courts of law.

3. Nurtured / Induced Entanglements. *(Slowly cultivated, disguised as care).* This is the most **dangerous and least obvious** category. These entanglements are relationally appealing, framed as love, mentorship, protection, or guidance, built incrementally, reinforced by praise or reassurance. Characteristics include words like, *"You're special." "God connected us." "You need covering." "I'll help you decide." "Stay close to me."*

Examples: Spiritual leaders cultivating dependency. This can even happen in a church, so you must discern every *spirit*. It may look like parents subtly discouraging independence. Children who are born into families that are spiritually entangled. Parents or mentors who never release. Partners who position themselves as necessary. *Consent is present, but informed consent is not.* That's why people feel confused rather than rebellious when trying to leave.

Freedom looks like naming the dynamic, Reclaiming agency, Relearning decision-making, Allowing grief without self-blame. If this has ever happened to you, don't blame yourself. Don't even blame others excessively. And, don't give up. You can honestly say, *"This wasn't my fault, but it is my responsibility now." "I wasn't stupid — I was shaped." "I can leave without hatred."*

Not all entanglements are entered the same way. Therefore, they are not exited the same way.

4. Forced Entanglements especially include slavery. There are 25 to 40 million slaves in the world, even today. **Forced Entanglements** like human trafficking, debt bondage, forced labor, domestic servitude, sexual exploitation and child soldiers. Slavery is a total loss of agency. It is coercion by force, threat, or deprivation. It is control over labor, body, movement, and decision-making. It creates the inability to exit without harm. That is the purest form of forced entanglement.

Slavery and Human Trafficking are totalizing systems of control. Some entanglements are enforced through violence, threat, deprivation, or captivity. In these cases, agency is removed, consent is impossible, and responsibility lies entirely with the oppressor. Freedom from such entanglements often requires rescue, legal intervention, and long-term restoration — not repentance or willpower. Not all entanglements are only spiritual; some are criminal.

On deliverance ground, there are reports of these very kinds of entanglements and even sexual slavery in the spirit realm. This is very real to the victim and there must be deliverance to be free from it.

I see entanglement as a hot pepper speed of double Dutch jump rope where the person can't stop jumping and they can't get out either because they may surely trip and fall. Constant motion. Still trying. They're not "choosing badly" — they're busy surviving the rhythm that they have no control over. Speed creates dependency. The ropes are moving fast. Stopping feels impossible. Thinking slows down or is even impossible. Instinct replaces reflection. That's exactly how entanglements work: *"I'll deal with this later, but right now, I just have to keep going."*

Momentum enforces the captivity.

There is fear of exit. The person knows that one wrong move will lead to a fall. It will lead to embarrassment, injury, exposure, collapse, or even death. So, they keep jumping, even when exhausted. This explains why people stay in dysfunctional relationships, abusive spiritual systems, financial traps, and enmeshments. It's not because they like it, but because the cost of stopping looks worse than the cost of continuing. They could be born into this, groomed into it, and it is all they know. From the outside it looks like choice, participation, even enjoyment, but that's not really what's happening. On the inside it's about fear, adrenaline, timing and vigilance.

Entanglement creates procedural memory, not just belief. When someone lives inside an entanglement long enough, the body learns it. This isn't ideology. It's neuromuscular conditioning. Like our example of double-Dutch at high speed, the body learns timing before the mind understands rhythm, stopping feels dangerous even when the ropes slow, stillness feels wrong, silence feels unsafe, and choice feels delayed.

Even when the external pressure eases, the internal rhythm continues. That's muscle memory. A person may reach for permission even when none is required. They may feel anxious when not consulted or consulting. They may over-explain decisions, default to appeasement, stay busy to avoid stillness, mistake calm for danger, or confuse autonomy with abandonment. They're no longer responding to the current situation. They're responding to a remembered one.

"Just leave" doesn't work; how can they *just leave?* Leaving removes the ropes, but muscle memory keeps the jumper moving. That's why people: leave a controlling church but still feel guilty. They may exit an enmeshed family but feel disoriented. They could break a dependency but feel unsafe alone. They could stop calling the authority but feel "off." The entanglement ended externally, but it's still alive somatically, inwardly.

Deliverance and unbraiding is not necessarily instant or all at once. Sometimes it must be slow and deliberate. You don't retrain muscle memory with insight alone. unbraiding requires slowing the pace, tolerating stillness, practicing decision-making, sitting with uncertainty, letting the body learn safety again, replacing reaction with presence.

This is why Wisdom says, *"Stand still and see."* Stillness isn't passive. It's retraining. Some entanglements survive not because they are enforced, but because the body remembers how to move inside them.

Inherited entanglements may happen when parents just teach their children to *go along with the get along?* This is one of the quietest and most powerful transmission mechanisms of entanglement. Inherited entanglements are taught, not chosen. Most inherited entanglements are passed down through training, not instruction. Parents rarely say, "Here is how to lose yourself." They say, "Don't rock the boat." "That's just how they are." "Be the bigger person." Keep the peace." "It's not worth it." "Family is family." "We don't talk about that."

God joins bodies in covenant, not consciences in captivity. People often excuse entanglement by saying, *"We're married." "We're family." "We're close."*

Genesis answers that before sin ever appears.: Union is holy. Fusion is not. If even marriage requires leaving and limits union to the flesh, then any bond that forbids separation or governs the soul is operating outside God's design.

What they're actually teaching is: *"Your comfort matters less than the system's stability."* That's the inheritance. *Go along to get along* is a survival strategy, not a virtue. The children? They are not weak; they are adapting.

Over time, the child internalizes a rule set, "My needs are disruptive." "Truth causes trouble." "Silence keeps me safe." "Belonging requires shrinking." "Distance equals danger."

Those rules don't disappear in adulthood. They show up as difficulty setting boundaries, fear of disagreement, over-functioning, chronic guilt, loyalty conflicts, paralysis around decisions, tolerance of dysfunction.

That's not personality; that's training.

This is inherited rather than healed. Parents who teach "go along to get along" often learned it themselves, survived by it, never had the chance to unlearn it, mistake endurance for Wisdom. So, they pass it on, not out of malice, but out of unexamined survival logic.

Spiritually, inherited entanglements have a real cost. They weaken discernment, confuse peace with avoidance, equate obedience with righteousness, frame silence as maturity, discourage moral courage. People raised this way often struggle to hear God clearly, not because God is silent, but because they were trained not to trust their own internal signals.

Some entanglements are inherited through training. Go along to *get along* teaches peacekeeping, not peacemaking. Entanglement can absolutely look and feel like a siege, and *self-siege* is one of the most accurate ways to describe what happens after the original external pressure is gone.

A siege is containment. Movement is restricted. resources are rationed. exits are watched. time is weaponized. exhaustion is the strategy. The goal isn't immediate destruction, it's wear-down until surrender.

Entanglement becomes an external siege that leads to an internalized siege. Most entanglements begin with something external. It can be a person, a system, a family dynamic, a spiritual authority, a financial dependency, or a survival context.

Over time, the external force doesn't need to stay. The rules get internalized. The person begins to monitor themselves, restrict themselves, anticipate consequences, self-censor, self-limit, self-police. That's when it becomes self-siege.

In practice, self-siege looks like a person may block their own options before others do, shut down impulses toward freedom, ration joy, rest, or pleasure, distrust stillness, avoid visibility, pre-emptively say "no" to themselves, assume scarcity even in abundance, live as if consequences are imminent. No guards are present, no walls are visible, but movement still feels impossible.

Self-siege is so effective because it masquerades as prudence, humility, maturity, spirituality, responsibility, and realism. The person isn't being attacked, they are containing themselves for safety. And often they believe that this is just how life is. Self-siege is muscle memory at the strategic level; the body remembers scarcity, punishment, backlash, loss, exposure and then governs itself according to that memory knowledge.

So, it maintains siege conditions even when resources exist, exits are open, danger has passed, authority is gone, permission is no longer needed. The siege continues because it once worked.

Self-siege explains why people remain bound without oppressors, live small without threat, silence themselves without command, delay obedience indefinitely, confuse safety with obedience, call restriction "wisdom"

It is the caged bird that remains in the cage even when the doors are open. They are not disobedient; they are contained.

THE 5-THREADS OF ENTANGLEMENT

Entanglements are never formed instantly; they braid. **Thread 1 — Proximity.** Repeated exposure. Being in the same environment repeatedly.

Thread 2 — Vulnerability. You shared something intimate too early or too deep.

Thread 3 — Expectation. They assume a role in your life.

Thread 4 — Emotional Transfer. You feel their feelings or their spiritual weight.

Thread 5 — Access. They gain entry into your inner world. When all five threads are present, the knot solidifies.

Entanglements form when **five threads** get braided together: They gain access to parts of your inner world that were never meant for them. **Once all five threads weave together, the entanglement is "locked."**

Knots do not form instantly; they form **gradually**, one thread at a time, one access point at a time, one micro-moment at a time. No one gets entangled from a single conversation. No one gets knotted from one encounter. No one becomes spiritually foggy because of one moment.

Entanglements form through **accumulation**, not impact. Thread after thread after thread… until movement becomes restricted, emotions become confused, and discernment becomes compromised.

This chapter reveals the **five threads** that weave an entanglement.

THE FIVE THREADS OF ENTANGLEMENT

Every knot — no matter how emotional, spiritual, accidental, or subtle — is formed through these **five threads**:

1. **Proximity**
2. **Vulnerability**
3. **Expectation**
4. **Emotional Transfer**
5. **Access**

If even **three** of these threads are present, an entanglement begins to form. If **all five** are present, the knot locks. Let's break down each thread with deep clarity.

THREAD 1 — PROXIMITY

"Proximity creates familiarity, and familiarity creates openings." You cannot become tangled with someone you never encounter. Proximity is the **first open door**, because proximity creates shared environment, repeated exposure, subtle connection, ongoing awareness, mutual acknowledgment. Proximity isn't intimacy, but the enemy doesn't need intimacy. He only needs access.

Proximity can happen through work, ministry, online interactions, social circles, family systems, routines, shared spaces, and even in spiritual communities. Perhaps especially in spiritual communities because you let your guard down thinking you are in a "safe" environment.

Proximity creates the illusion that the connection was "meant to be," when in reality, it was simply **geography**. Proximity alone doesn't entangle — but it lays the **foundation** for the knot. It gives the enemy a place to drop the next thread.

THREAD 2 — VULNERABILITY

Every entanglement begins with an unguarded moment. Vulnerability is not confession. Vulnerability is exposure. And that exposure is of emotion, weakness, fear, longing, hurt, confusion, rejection, loneliness, a secret, a wound.

The moment you feel "seen" by the wrong person, the enemy drops a thread. This vulnerability may be intentional (you opened up), accidental (something slipped out), emotional (your heart was open), spiritual (your guard was down), atmospheric (you were tired, stressed, grieving).

Vulnerability becomes a thread when someone steps in too closely, someone responds too intimately, someone mirrors your emotions, someone takes advantage of your openness, someone ties themselves into your pain. This thread is thin — but powerful.

It gives a person emotional weight they were never meant to carry.

THREAD 3 — EXPECTATION

"Expectation binds without covenant." This is the thread nobody sees forming. It happens when either person begins to assume: a role, a place, a connection, a significance, a responsibility, a bond a future, a meaning, a position, Expectation can form from a single meaningful conversation. a moment of comfort. a period of closeness. a crisis. a shared vulnerability. perceived empathy. spiritual guidance. emotional mirroring. habitual checking-in. unspoken agreements.

Expectations create invisible contracts. Contracts that say, "You owe me communication." "You owe me clarity. "You owe me empathy." "You owe me attention." "I matter to you more than others." "We have something."

Expectation is the thread that creates emotional obligation. Suddenly you feel guilty pulling back. You feel wrong not responding. You feel uneasy when they're upset. You feel responsible for their feelings.

Expectation is the most deceptive thread because it feels like connection but it functions like control.

THREAD 4 — EMOTIONAL TRANSFER

"You begin to feel what is not yours." This is the supernatural thread. This is where entanglement becomes spiritual. Emotional transfer is when your emotions respond to THEIR emotional state.

This can feel like sudden heaviness, sadness that isn't yours, regret that isn't yours, longing that isn't yours, guilt that isn't yours, anxiety that isn't yours, intrusive thoughts, random emotional waves, mental noise, unexplained burden.

This is the thread that causes dream access, atmospheric shifts, prophetic confusion, spiritual misreading, emotional empathy overload, internal conflict.

This is not "being sensitive; this is being entangled. You are carrying emotional energy that does not belong to you. It does not come from within you — it comes from connection to them.

Emotional transfer is the thread that tightens the knot.

THREAD 5 — ACCESS

"Access is the anchor thread. The knot cannot form without it." Access is the ability to influence your emotions, atmosphere, decisions, peace, mood, spiritual clarity, identity.

Access can come from communication, spiritual exchange, emotional dependence, physical presence, conversation history, digital contact, dream intrusion, unguarded moments, open spiritual doors, unclosed gateways after conflict. unhealed wounds they tapped into

Access is not them speaking; access is you responding. Access is not them reaching — access is you receiving. Access is not them communicating, access is your spirit opening.

When access is given, boundaries weaken, clarity fades, discernment dulls, expectations grow, emotional threads deepen, spiritual influence increases. Access is the final thread, because access is what allows the knot to close.

When a person has access to your spirit, they have access to your clarity. When they have access to your clarity, they have access to your decisions.

When they have access to your decisions, they have access to your direction. This is why knots feel so powerful. They sit at the intersection of emotion, spirit, identity, and assignment.

When all five threads are present, the knot locks.

1. Proximity → They're around
2. Vulnerability → They gain insight
3. Expectation → A role forms
4. Emotional Transfer → Their feelings enter your space
5. Access → You begin to respond from entanglement, not discernment

This is how knots form--, not loudly, Not dramatically, and not obviously, but quietly, incrementally, thread by thread. Once formed, a knot can control emotions, reactions, decision, your peace, your dreams, clarity, spiritual intuition, your boundaries, your atmosphere, focus and pace.

That knot did not start as a knot; it started as a thread. To be dismantled, they must be **unbraided thread by thread.**

DECLARATION

I identify every thread — proximity, vulnerability, expectation, emotional transfer, and access.
I withdraw the threads one by one. I reclaim my emotions. I reclaim my clarity.
I reclaim my atmosphere.
Every thread begins to loosen.

COUNTERFEIT CORDS

Every God-ordained connection has *marks. If you do not see these marks then suspect counterfeit.*

Clarity is a God-cord.

Everyone who sits around from day to day and week to week trying to figure out what *"they"* meant, what their intentions really are, or why they are not treating you as you should be treated--, that's not God. That is not a Godly connection. Peace should be plainly evident; As well, mutuality, honor, alignment with God. Strength, security, and purpose. If any or all of these markers are missing, then God is not in it. If God is not in it, then why are you?

God doesn't play. God doesn't waste your time. God brings righteousness, Peace, and joy in the Holy Ghost into your life, not guesswork, time wastage and trauma. And there is nothing you can do to change the marks on a person who has marked themselves with unholy behaviors. They have to decide on their own; you can not rehabilitate them.

Every counterfeit connection has *symptoms such as*: guilt, pull, pressure, confusion, intrusion, obsession, Emotional imbalance, and identity distortion.

What God binds brings order.

What the enemy entangles brings disorder.

Some knots don't look like knots at first. They look like cords. They know you won't buy that; so they step to you subtle, like the Serpent, masquerading as something *godly*, something *intentional* and *meaningful*.

They look like what you WISH the connection were. And how do they know what you wished for. Well, your big mouth for one; you told even one somebody, whether they asked or not. You told a whole lot of people over the years. You told the impersonator. Ladies: when you meet a new guy and you go down the list of what you are looking for, don't you think they will pretend to be that thing that you're looking for if they are trying to tie you up, bind you up, or get something out of you? And, *familiar* and *monitoring spirits* have been with you all your life: they know what you look it, what you like, what you eat, drink and what you do when no one is looking or when you think no one is looking. They know your spec and will dress up anything and anyone to look like, sound like and temporarily be like just what you're looking for, if you are an enemy target.

The enemy never shows up with chaos in his hands. He shows up offering **counterfeit cords** — connections that mimic God's pattern, but are powered by the wrong *spirit*, the wrong motives, or the wrong alignment.

This chapter reveals the **three primary counterfeit cords** that form entanglements:

1. **The Cord of Emotional Seduction**
2. **The Cord of Spiritual Confusion**
3. **The Cord of Identity Distortion**

These three cords braid together to create the **entangled knot**.

1. THE CORD OF EMOTIONAL SEDUCTION

"It feels like closeness, but it functions like control."

Emotional seduction has NOTHING to do with romance or sexuality. It has EVERYTHING to do with attention, energy, access, and pull. Emotional seduction is when someone gains influence over you through attention, flattery, vulnerability exchanges, shared weakness, emotional mirroring, empathy traps, subtle dependency, trauma sharing too early, making you feel needed, or creating emotional urgency.

This is the kind of counterfeit cord that says things like, "You understand me like no one else." "I can't talk to anyone but you." "You're the only person who gets me." "I feel so safe with you." "You're different." Now not only are these soap-opera and movie lines, they are definitely *player* lines. So, learn how to spot a *player*. This is not gender specific. These lines feel flattering, but they are **hooks**. They bypass logic. They bypass boundaries. They bypass discernment.

The Bible warns us about flattery and flatterers.

A man that flattereth his neighbour spreadeth a net for his feet. (Proverbs 29:5)

Emotional seduction doesn't ask for connection; it creates a connection you feel responsible to maintain. You begin to feel emotionally obligated, guilty for pulling back, responsible for their emotions, afraid of disappointing them, or overly bonded, internally conflicted. This is not love, attraction, or friendship. It is a **counterfeit cord.**

It mimics the emotional intimacy of a God-ordained bond — but without covenant, boundaries, clarity, or purpose. The function of emotional seduction is simple. Create emotional dependence where God never placed emotional assignment. That dependence becomes the first thread of entanglement.

2. THE CORD OF SPIRITUAL CONFUSION

When someone's presence disrupts your discernment, it is never God. **Never**. This cord does not form through emotions, but through spiritual energy, atmosphere, and unseen influence. You can be spiritually entangled with someone even if you never dated them, you don't desire them, you don't even LIKE them, you don't talk often, you barely know them personally. Because spiritual entanglements do not form through compatibility, they form through **exchange.** And exchange can happen in prayer, vulnerability, undue influence, "prophetic words" given too soon, spiritual dependence, mentorship without boundaries, prayers of agreement you should have never agreed to, spiritual curiosity, shared spiritual weakness, manipulative counsel, unauthorized spiritual covering.

The Cord of Spiritual Confusion produces fog, heaviness, disrupted sleep, dream access, intruding thoughts, atmospheric shift, inability to hear God clearly, strange emotional weight, spiritual silence when dealing with them, and confusion about who they are to you. This cord mimics **spiritual connection**, but lacks God's order and God's Peace. It feels "deep," but it's not spiritual depth, it's spiritual interference. It feels "prophetic," but it's not revelation; it's intrusion. It feels "familiar," but it's not covenant, it's entanglement.

This is the cord that causes people to mistake distraction for destiny, interference for intimacy, spiritual weight for spiritual significance, confusion for chemistry, familiarity for favor. And this is the cord that opens the dream realm.

We'll deal with dream entanglements later, but hear this: If someone's spiritual presence makes you confused instead of clear, you are dealing with a counterfeit cord. If you have weird, unusual dreams when someone new enters your life, suspect dream entanglements.

3. THE CORD OF IDENTITY DISTORTION

"This is the most dangerous cord because it ties into who you are." Identity distortion is when someone begins to influence your sense of self. If you are struggling every day to assert your identity—who you know yourself to be, or who you know God has told you that you are, that's a real fight. Identity distortion affects your stated and implied boundaries, your decisions and calling. Your emotional responses, your self-worth, your inner voice and your inner court positioning

This cord does NOT hook into your emotions; it hooks into your assignment, your purpose, and your identity. You start asking yourself things like: "What will they think?" "Are they disappointed?" "Do I owe them a response?" "Am I supposed to help them?" "Should I change this because of them?" "Can I move forward without them?"

When someone begins to subtly influence your identity YOU HAVE BEEN TIED. Careful here if you are one to try to become someone else to hook or please a person. Change your hair because they like it this way. Lose weight, gain weight, the way you dress. Changing many things about yourself including your personality—this is most likely identity distortion.

Identity distortion cords form when a person assumes a place in your life they were never given. Begins to "read" your calling. positions themselves as your emotional compass. speaks into you without authorization. attaches themselves to your purpose. claims a spiritual role in your destiny. tries to "father," "mother," "pastor," or "mentor" you without being asked. creates invisible, unspoken obligations. This is the cord that binds your **spirit**, not your emotions. Identity distortion is the cord that makes you neglect yourself, silence your voice, pause your purpose. question your value, minimize your authority, misplace your loyalty.

It is the most dangerous of the three counterfeit cords because it shifts the inner throne. Suddenly, God is not the center. YOU aren't the center, the knot is.

THE THREE CORDS TOGETHER FORM THE ENTANGLED KNOT

When all three counterfeit cords braid, the knot becomes powerful, restrictive, draining, controlling, confusing. There is power when two agree. When three agree there is even more strength, only this time to the negative. Not only that it becomes spiritually invasive and identity-altering.

The enemy doesn't need you to sin. He only needs you to be tangled. Because tangled people don't move well, don't discern well, don't hear well, don't choose well, don't protect themselves well and they do not progress well.

A tangled Christian is a distracted Christian. A distracted Christian is a delayed Christian. A delayed Christian is a vulnerable Christian. A vulnerable Christian is a misaligned Christian. That is the strategy.

That is the design. Not to break you; to bind you. Not to hurt you, but to hijack you. Not to destroy your faith. To derail your clarity.

The tool isn't always trauma, sometimes the tool is a **cord** that looks Godly, feels meaningful, and seems innocent. But it's not. It's counterfeit, and counterfeit cords always end in constriction.

The relationship between the 5 Threads and the 3 Cords. **The 5 threads are how the entanglement forms. The 3 cords are what the entanglement** *becomes*. Threads describe process. Cords describe result. Threads are gradual; cords are structural. Threads are the small openings. Cords are the counterfeit bonds created once enough threads braid together. Threads create the opening; Cords create the bondage. Threads are the pathway; Cords are the knot.

Once enough threads exist, they braid into one of the three counterfeit cords. When all three cords are present, the knot is complete.

Entanglements do not begin as cords. They begin as threads. Threads are the small, repeated openings that seem harmless at first. Proximity, vulnerability, expectation, emotional transfer, and access. These threads do not bind by themselves. But when enough of them braid together, they form something stronger.

Threads create the conditions. Cords create the bond. Once the threads have done their work, the entanglement no longer feels like a series of moments. It feels like a relationship, a connection, a weight, or a pull. That is when the threads have braided into one of the three counterfeit cords: emotional seduction, spiritual confusion, or identity distortion.

When all three cords are present, the knot tightens. Threads = how it starts. Cords = what it turns into. Knot = what happens when all cords are present.

No one is tied by a cord they did not first allow as a thread.

DECLARATION

I break every counterfeit cord —
of emotional seduction, spiritual confusion, and identity distortion. I refuse every false bond.
I reject every imitated connection. I renounce every unauthorized attachment. The knot is exposed.
The cords are cut. I return to clarity.

PROPHETIC & SENSITIVE PEOPLE GET ENTANGLED EASILY

Prophetic and spiritually sensitive people are favorite targets. They live with their **spirit exposed**, not exposed in a dangerous way, but in a *perceptive* and *awake* way. They are emotionally open, spiritually perceptive, atmosphere-aware, deeply intuitive, soft around the edges, and naturally empathic. Prophetic people are wired for connection and to absorb information. They are wired to read what is unsaid, including motivations and wired to feel what is invisible. Their strength is sensitivity.

But their vulnerability is **also sensitivity.** And this is why the enemy uses entanglements as a targeted attack strategy against folks, and especially against prophetic people.

This chapter explains why.

1. PROPHETIC PEOPLE FEEL (sense) BEFORE THEY THINK. Prophetic wiring is sensory first. You *feel* things before you interpret them. Jesus said, someone touched me. Virtue flowed out of me.

You *sense* things before you understand them. You *pick up* things before you analyze them.

This means you detect spiritual currents. you absorb emotional information. you notice subtle shifts. you feel inner reactions. you internalize atmospheres. Herein is the danger. Prophetic people can confuse feeling with meaning.

You feel a pull; you think it's purpose. You feel a weight; you think it's responsibility. You feel a connection; you think it's covenant. You feel a stirring, maybe that's God highlighting the person. You feel drawn, without discerning this *'drawing'* anointing, you may think it's destiny.

If prophets confuse discernment data with divine direction, entanglements will exploit that.

Intercessors, many times, absorb what they should observe. Intercessors are spiritually porous. They are designed to pick up burdens, sense weight, and feel atmospheres. When untrained, intercessors can absorb emotions, internalize confusion, take on false burdens, and step into dynamics not assigned to them. Often, they feel responsible for people they're not called to, and carry weights that don't belong to them. The devil may use this to dump loads on them.

Owner of evil load, take your load, I will no longer carry it, in the Name of Jesus.

Entanglements hook intercessors through compassion. They show you a wound. You feel it. You desire to help. You spiritually lean in. A thread forms. False intercession is one of the biggest gateways to soul knots.

4. FEELERS HAVE SOFT BOUNDARIES. Feelers sense everything: moods, shifts, tones, undercurrents, motives, spiritual shadows, emotional climates. Feelers love deeply and intuitively. But feelers also overextend, take responsibility, merge easily, trust emotional familiarity, misread their own empathy as divine assignment. Feelers do not fall into entanglement they **slide**. Without noticing, choosing, or intending.

Entanglement is the enemy's favorite trap for feelers.

5. SEERS NOTICE THE PERSON'S SPIRIT — NOT THEIR DANGER Seers look **through** people, not at them. They see potential, calling, gifts, wounds, destiny, possibility. But this makes seers vulnerable. Because while seers see a person's spirit, they sometimes ignore the person's behavior, their impact, or their effect on the seer's clarity.

Seers get entangled because they see the healed version of the person. they see the potential. They see who the person *could* be. Through the eyes of Grace and agape Love, they sense destiny, not dysfunction. But anointing does not override boundaries.

6. PROPHETIC PEOPLE MISTAKE SPIRITUAL NOISE FOR SPIRITUAL DEPTH. This is a sharp truth. Prophetic people often mistake emotional intensity, spiritual sensitivity, dream activity, energetic pull, supernatural interference …for God highlighting something.

But in reality, sometimes activity is not God; it's warfare. Sometimes intensity is not confirmation; it's conflict. Sometimes dreams are not destiny; they are merely a distraction. Prophetic people get tangled because they mistake spiritual activity for spiritual purpose.

7. THEY ARE TARGETS BECAUSE THEIR ASSIGNMENT IS HIGH-VALUE

The enemy targets prophets, seers, intercessors, dreamers, and feelers with entanglements because they hear God clearly when unentangled. They move fast when unburdened. They discern sharply when undistracted. They are influential in the spirit. They break cycles when free. They expose darkness when clear. They are spiritually disruptive to the kingdom of darkness

Entanglements are assignment-sabotage. The enemy cannot stop a prophet from hearing, so he knots the prophet's clarity.

He cannot stop an intercessor from praying so he knots the intercessor's emotions. He cannot stop a dreamer from receiving, so he knots the dream gate. He cannot stop a discerner from seeing, so he knots the identity. He cannot destroy the assignment, so he knots the assignment path.

8. SENSITIVE PEOPLE REACT IN THE SPIRIT FASTER THAN IN THE SOUL. Sensitive believers react spiritually BEFORE they react emotionally. They sense spiritually BEFORE they interpret mentally. They feel spiritually BEFORE they understand logically. So, when a knot forms, they feel heaviness, fog, pull, discomfort, then they respond. When something resonates it sparks their curiosity and send them into urgency--, sometimes without knowing WHY.

This leads to self-doubt "Am I too sensitive?". "Am I imagining this?" "Why does this affect me?" "I can't explain it, but something's happening."

This confusion tightens the knot.

THE GOOD NEWS: THESE SAME QUALITIES MAKE Those with these spiritual gifts EXCELLENT AT UNBRAIDING

The enemy targeted your sensitivity, but God entrusts sensitivity. The same traits that made you entangle easily, make you UNBRAID quickly. Feelers sense when release begins. Intercessors pray their way out. Seers recognize spiritual interference. Dreamers close dream gates. And prophetic people obey very quickly when clarity hits.

Your sensitivity is your superpower, once unentangled. Not to simplify the process but it is as though what you're going through is **practice**. Now you can help others get out of their tangled messes.

> Blessed be the Lord my strength which teacheth my hands to war, and my fingers to fight:
>
> My goodness, and my fortress; my high tower, and my deliverer; my shield, and he in whom I trust; who subdueth my people under me. (Psalm 144:1-2)

THE SHIFT: SENSITIVE PEOPLE NEED SKILL, NOT HARDNESS

You do NOT need to toughen up. You do NOT need to become guarded. You do NOT need to suppress your gift. You do NOT need to shut down emotionally.

You need knowledge, awareness, holy boundaries, spiritual hygiene, assignment clarity, internal sovereignty, and self-governance.

Once trained, sensitive people become the most untouchable, most clear, most accurate, most protected Believers on Earth. They feel the knot forming even before it tightens. They sense the thread before it wraps. They detect intrusion before it settles. They know when someone's spirit is out of order before entanglement happens.

Your sensitivity was never the problem; God made you exactly right. The problem was more likely your lack of language and strategy was. *Now*? You have both.

DECLARATION

Lord, I declare that:

My sensitivity is not weakness — it is holy intelligence.
I am spiritually aware, not spiritually vulnerable.
I am prophetic, not porous.
I am discerning, not destabilized.
Every knot that used my sensitivity is breaking.
Every misuse of my gift is ending.
I stand clear, sovereign, aligned, and untangled.

In the Name of Jesus. Amen.

DREAM KNOTS

Dreamers are open during the night watch. Dreamers have open spiritual gates while asleep. Their subconscious is a landing pad for revelation, instruction, intrusion and other spiritual activity, visitation, which is not always good --. It is also a place for warning, and alignment. It goes the gamut.

But if the wrong person has emotional, spiritual, or atmospheric threads with a dreamer... here we go. They may appear in dreams because the dreamer's spirit is open. The knot created a night-gate. The dreamer is spiritually sensitive, and their subconscious is highly receptive.

This is not romantic. Nor is it prophetic. It is not destiny; it is intrusion, and that is a marker and a symptom of entanglement. Dreamers get entangled deeper because their dream realm, unknowingly participates in the knot.

DREAM KNOTS: *Some say, let us dance. Others say, let us go. But first—let us listen for the knots that visit us in the night.*

There are tangles we tie without knowing. Threads pulled in silence. Loops that form while we sleep, when the soul begins speaking in its own strange grammar. You know them. The dreams that leave you heavy. The faces you haven't seen in years, suddenly waiting at the edge of your bed. The hallway with too many doors. The voice that says nothing, but still wakes you.

We call them dream knots; Not because they are puzzles, not because they need to be solved. But because they hold. They linger. They whisper of something unfinished— a gesture that was never made, a word never spoken, a version of you that still wants to be met.

Dream knots are where entanglement begins. Before you try to undo the visible threads, before you trace the tension in your waking life, listen to what you've carried into your sleep. in the half-light, in liminal hours, in the places you thought you'd forget. Where the knots hum softly beneath the surface.

A teenager said she braided her younger sister's hair, but it was a struggle, so I said, when my little sisters resisted (unbraiding, detangling or knot removal) we would just 'do their hair' while they were asleep. They'd wake up in the am and just brush their hair, because it was already done. (This intrigued her, but she's 15, so there's that.)

Some knots are not metaphors; some are found in the morning mirror — sudden tangles, spirals in the hair, snarls formed while we slept.

What if the same could be done for the knots inside us? What if healing didn't always require permission — only tenderness?

Is this something dark and spiritual? It *can be*. In spiritual, folkloric, and even esoteric traditions, hair often represents Memory (it grows with us, holds time). It represents Identity. Hair represents connection to spirit or ancestral line. It represents protection and power. Think of Samson and Native American hair customs.

In Japan, a phenomenon is reported where people go to sleep at night and wake up with their hair in knots the next morning. The hair is not merely tangled; it is in knots.

So, when hair tangles in sleep, even if you are sleeping on beauty silk pillowcases, it can symbolize emotional or psychic entanglement. It may reflect dream interference, unresolved energies, or ancestral tension. In some belief systems (Japan included), it's associated with wandering *spirits*, karmic entanglement, or subconscious knots forming or surfacing

The hair is one's glory.

So, let's look at tangled hair.

1. Hair as a symbol

Across Scripture and many cultures, hair carries symbolic meaning. Symbol does *not* mean superstition; it means representation. Biblically and culturally, hair has been associated with Glory, honor, identity, time and continuity, since it grows with us. Hair can be symbolic of covenant or consecration, as in the Nazarite vow. It is representative of strength delegated by God, not generated by the person.

When Paul says that *a woman's hair is her glory,* (1 Cor. 11), he is speaking symbolically about covering, honor, distinction, and visible identity.

Hair can function as a metaphor for personal history, identity, continuity, emotional accumulation, or relational threads.

2. Hair tangling in sleep can be physically normal. Period. Symbolically, however (especially in dreams or interpretation), it can *represent* unresolved emotional threads, thoughts looping overnight, stress surfacing when conscious control is lowered relational complexity. identity strain. "things crossing that shouldn't.

This happened because of a beauty curse or *spirits* tangled your hair. Scripture never teaches that but folklore and on deliverance ground we've seen and heard of such things.

3. Folklore and esoteric traditions such as Japanese folklore, ancestral beliefs, esoteric symbolism, wandering spirits, karmic entanglement. Those systems do interpret physical phenomena as spiritual interference.

Folklore explains experience; Scripture interprets reality. Folklore may be interesting, poetic, or psychologically revealing, but it is not authoritative theology.

Tangled or even knotted hair does not necessarily mean there's been a spiritual attack. Knots do not necessarily mean there's been demonic manipulation, or spiritual contamination. No matter the cause or whether or not you can "prove it", it never hurts to pray. If you dream it or you get a knowing in your spirit; it never hurts to pray.

There is a phenomenon called backbiting which I mention it in another book entitled, **Backbiters** where evil is cast behind one's back, usually while they know nothing about it, and too often by barbers or hairstylists some of whom engage in dark arts. By no means am I saying all or a predominance of hair care professionals dabble in the dark arts.

It is also known that any part of you can represent you on an evil altar. In many cultures, it starts with the placenta or anything that contains your DNA can be used—even your hair or the dirt off the soles of your shoes--, almost anything. So, stay prayed up and you don't have to worry. It is also known that some who employ the dark arts go to hair salons an the like to "buy" hair that has been cut there, and they pay the person who cut the hair. None of this is to stress you; it is to encourage you to walk upright before the Lord, pray, and stay prayed up.

Samson's hair was not knotted, but it was manipulated. It was removed while he slept, through betrayal resulting in loss of consecrated strength, not identity. Samson's story is not about entanglement. It's about covenant violation and removal of consecration. If hair symbolized *identity*, Samson didn't become confused. If hair symbolized *glory*, his glory wasn't tangled — it was taken. If hair symbolized *power*, the power was withdrawn, not corrupted. That distinction alone dismantles a lot of speculative teaching. But think about it, where was Samson's head? In Delilah's lap.

The text (2 Samuel 18) Absalom is described earlier as having extraordinarily beautiful hair. hair that was so heavy it was *weighed* annually. Later, while fleeing, "Absalom happened to meet the servants of David. Absalom was riding on his mule, and the mule went under the thick branches of a great oak, and his head caught fast in the oak, and he was suspended between heaven and earth…" (2 Sam. 18:9)

The Hebrew suggests his hair was implicated — the very thing he was known for. Absalom's hair represents his beauty and glory. Unlike Samson, Absalom's hair was not consecration. It was self-glory. Absalom's defining traits: obsession with appearance charisma without submission. ambition without patience. rebellion against rightful authority. identity built on admiration.

His hair symbolized cultivated image, personal glory, public appeal, pride carefully maintained. So, when his hair catches in the tree, the text is making a statement.

Trees in Scripture often represent lineage, authority, established order, rootedness, and God-ordained structure.

Absalom is literally caught between heaven and earth. His behavior in this passage shows us that he was not submitted to God. not aligned with rightful authority, self-exalted, suspended by his own vain glory, pride, disobedience, and rebellion. That's not spiritual attack; that's consequence. This was entanglement only in the sense that Absalom willingly agreed with vanity and pride to form these 'knots' in his soul.

Notice the contrast, Samson's glory was removed due to covenant violation. Absalom's God-given beauty and glory entangled due to pride and rebellion. In both cases hair represents *glory*. For Samson, loss comes through sleep and trusting the wrong person, someone playing in his hair. For Absalom loss came because of inattention and flight. The issue is alignment, not identity. Each case supports: glory mishandled, authority rejected, self-image becoming a snare.

What we use to exalt ourselves can become what entangles us.

If Absalom's inner life had not already been *knotted*, his outer glory would not have become a snare. The text is inviting us to see this: his glory was overgrown, his identity was over-invested in appearance, His life was overloaded with contradiction, His loyalties were crossed. His ambitions were misaligned. His heart was divided

So, when pressure came, nothing was free to move. That's what knots do: they reduce mobility. They convert beauty into liability. They turn flexibility into capture. Why would anyone want you captured or captive? The answer is always to steal, kill, or destroy.

Entanglements are illegal spiritual knots.

Entanglements form through repeated agreement. Knots form when traits reinforce each other. Beauty without order becomes risk. Strength without submission becomes vulnerability. Visibility without alignment becomes exposure. Absalom's internal disorder manifested externally when pressure came. Absalom was trapped by what had already intertwined within him. The knots that held Absalom were formed long before the branches touched his hair.

It's no coincidence that in many ghost stories (particularly in Japanese folklore), ghosts are depicted with long, tangled, unkempt hair. In that, hair becomes a visual metaphor for unrest. This could be a physical expression of a dream knot. It could be a signal that something is trying to surface, tighten, or be noticed.

Knots do not always form in the dream although they can because you are in the spirit at that time. Sometimes the body tells the story the dream couldn't finish.

Symbols can reveal truth without defining cause. the Holy Spirit can lead us into all Truth, so we should stay *prayed up* and always attuned to the Spirit of God. We weigh out with Wisdom all we see, hear, and have heard from others.

The act of *tending* to someone even when they resist — that's its own kind of entanglement. Transformation overnight. They wake up, and the tangle is gone. This is healing without conscious struggle.

No matter how tangled, entangled, or knotted, God heals by unbraiding entanglements. He cleanses what *touches* us, and He can restore our glory.

SPIRIT SPOUSE – SPIRIT CHILDREN

Spirit spouse and also *spirit children* are the fruit of spiritual entanglements. Many would argue that neither of these two things exist. If you have suffered under the oppression of either, you know that they do. These entanglements are very different because the fruit of them is evident to you to prove that there was or still is entanglement.

The way to be rid of these is first you have to get rid of the evidence. Does that mean you are guilty? Whether or not, you are made to look guilty. And when the evidence is presented, you yourself will either be shocked or tend to believe it yourself.

No, this is not like Genesis 6 where the fallen angels *went into* the daughters of men and created the giants of the Earth (Nephilim). *Spirit spouse* and *spirit children* are in the spirit realm only (usually) but they exist. You sense them, some say they hear them. Some dream of them--, often. Those who dream of being in the same family all the time and it's not your real life family – they say that's a *spirit spouse* and *spiritual children.* The purpose of *spirit spouse* is to ruin, block, or derail your marriage in the natural. The purpose of *spirit children* is to torment either you and or your real natural children.

Women have been reporting this since the beginning of time, yet many still say it is not real. There are as many as 30+ types of *spirit spouses* their designations are based on their source, where they come from or how they happen to be in someone's life. It's hard to digest how there are more than 30 types of a thing that *"doesn't exist."* Be sure you pray and ask God for yourself what may be going on in your own life or why you have repetitive dreams about a person or a family that you seem to be a part of.

(Read my book **Fantasy Spirit Spouse**, or any other *spirit spouse* books for more on this subject. Those books include prayers to be free of *spirit spouse* and *spirit children*. If this is real, and God will let you know, this would be the deepest form of spiritual entanglement.

Now, the results of having *spirit spouse* or *spirit children* can be seen or sensed in the natural. That does not mean that *spirit spouse* or *spirit children* 'come to life'. It's not like that, however some of the torment that people experience in real life is the result of having tormentors in the spirit realm. This can be simple or complex, depending on how you see it and who you are in the spirit. Part of getting out of these sexual types of spiritual entanglements is first to be rid of the fruit. As long as there is a spirit child around, the *spirit spouse* will remain.

OPPORTUNISTIC ONES

The opportunistic overpower others because they are "mystical" or "magical." They overpower because they understand human leverage and authority gaps. They don't usually attack strength. They exploit openness, dependency, loyalty, fear, and unfinished identity.

The common profile (Biblically and practically). These figures share several traits and can occupy a legitimate position.

- Laban: family elder, employer
- Pharaoh: ruler, provider of survival
- Saul: king, spiritual authority

They don't usually come as outsiders. They come as insiders, with standing.

They trade provision for control.

- Laban paid Jacob — but changed the wages.
- Pharaoh fed Israel — then enslaved them.
- Saul anointed David — then tried to own him.

The hook is not cruelty-- *at first*. It's access + benefit + obligation. Once provision is normalized, exit feels like betrayal.

They blur boundaries gradually. They don't dominate instantly. They extend favors, create emotional indebtedness, normalize overreach, redefine "loyalty." By the time resistance forms, the person is already *inside the system, their snare*. That's entanglement.

The opportunistic ones are threatened by autonomy. All three reacted violently when someone grew independent, received divine favor, outgrew the arrangement. Saul feared David's trajectory because it was greater than his and Saul could not stop it. People like this are not comforted by your affection. They are comforted by your containment.

ENTANGLEMENTS BY DARK METHODS

About "charms" and modalities. In Scripture, the primary mechanism is not charms — it is words, roles, and atmosphere. Even when occult practices exist in the Bible, they are secondary. They are unnecessary if authority over a person is established. However, those dark spiritual tricks can be employed by the opportunistic ones to take over another's agency.

.   Most real-world overpowering happens through speech, repetition, expectation, emotional scripting, spiritual language without consent. This is evil imaginations. Just as God created the Heavens and the Earth with words, the dark kingdom also uses words to do what they do.

Some people are especially vulnerable. Not because they're weak, but because they are conscientious, loyal, empathetic, spiritually open, unused to predatory authority. Predators prefer good people with poor boundaries, not fools.

The most dangerous controllers do not seize power; they are given it by people who mistake access for trust. Overpowering rarely feels like force at first. It feels like being chosen.

Biblically, God's response is not "fight harder." It is always distance, separation, relocation, new governance.

Jacob had to leave. Israel had to leave. David had to leave. Freedom did not come from confrontation. It came from disentanglement.

When talking about those who use the dark arts, I'm talking about those who, as they say are... people who just have a "*way*" about them, they are charismatic, charming. They have a *seducing spirit* about them and you may not realize that they do. They are the types who make you believe you are the only other person, or the only important person in the world. While you're with them.

People who *"have a way about them"* are skilled at influence, often unconsciously, sometimes intentionally. Charismatic people are good at setting emotional tone, holding attention, reading the room, mirroring what others want to feel.

The core mechanisms they use (often unknowingly) 1. Emotional attunement. They make people feel seen, chosen, understood, and significant. This creates rapid trust, which lowers discernment.

2. Confidence without accountability. They speak decisively about people, outcomes, and meaning.

Certainty is contagious, especially to the young, spiritually immature, to people who are still forming identity.

These types take narrative control. They tell stories that place themselves at the center. They make themselves the hero, rescuer, visionary, and misunderstood leader. People begin to borrow the narrative instead of thinking independently.

They are often familiar too fast. intense too soon. They want to make you trust them with their fake sincerity and warmth. They push past your boundaries and get very friendly, very quickly. They are emotionally engaging before consent is established. All the above initiate and accelerate entanglement.

Most real-world overpowering does not involve charms, rituals, or occult tools. It involves words, tone, repetition, expectation, spiritual language, social pressure, emotional leverage. But it depends on the culture you are born into or the one you live in.

The most affected by these dark practices are not foolish or weak people. No, it is thoughtful people, empathetic people, spiritually receptive people, loyal people, people who give the benefit of the doubt who could fall for these traps. It is intelligent people who just happen to be kind. Charismatic controllers prey on good faith, not stupidity.

Charisma becomes dangerous when it replaces another person's ability to govern themselves. Influence becomes control when consent is no longer required.

People who "have a way" are not powerful because they are special. They are powerful because others temporarily surrender their internal authority in the presence of confidence, warmth, or certainty. But sometimes people who have a way have that *way* because they are *charmed*. Without being prayed up, if you encounter a person who is charmed – charmed in anyway, their eyes, their smile, their words, their looks, you are at risk because spiritual power cannot be countered with flesh or will power, as some people believe. Some people use charms. While others believe that if they don't believe in such a thing it can't be true or it can't touch them.

Not so. Dark charms must be countered with a higher spiritual power: God's power. The natural man, in his flesh is no match for spiritual power of any kind. We need God 24/7. Period. If I were to tell you other than this, that would not be fair to you.

You may have heard a person say, *I don't know what it is, but when I look into his eyes*. Or, *that smile, I can't resist it*. (Wonder why.) When you find yourself doing what you would not do, giving up what you would not normally give up, agreeing to what you would not normally agree to, there may be a spiritual charge on the person or person making requests or demands of you. You MUST stay prayed up.

The first tiny agreement or concession is the first thread to a potential entanglement. That is what this book is about. Pharaoh, Laban, any manipulator, even those in real life in modern times can start out nice but they are confident because of who or what they serve. They are confident because they are empowered, but they have to follow the rules of the one(s) who empower them to have power over people and situations.

To be victorious over them, you must be upright and serving the One you serve because He is the greatest power, as long as you are all in and you invoke the power of Jehovah God, which is sometimes simple discernment that tells you, No, don't agree. Or, Go, get out of there. Entanglements start with a simple thread. Blocking that first thread is preventative and will save a world of hurt.

Pharaoh could not release Israel without unraveling the systems that sustained him. When obedience threatens another person's identity, economy, or power source, resistance escalates. This does not mean the believer is wrong; it means the entanglement is being exposed. God does not ask His people to fix the bindings of others. He calls them to move when released.

Some people resist your freedom not because they hate you, but because your obedience threatens what they are bound to. Entanglement on the throne produces bondage in the land.

FINANCIAL ENTANGLEMENTS

THE PROBLEM OF COMPETING HANDS

Entanglement occurs when more than one hand begins directing the same area of life. This is especially visible in finances. Competing hands and the cost of shared control could be why some people's money is blocked. Most entanglements do not begin with consent. They begin with assumption. Jurisdiction is often surrendered unknowingly, gradually, politely, in moments of need or convenience. No declaration is made. No agreement is signed. But authority shifts anyway.

Money requires clarity, direction, and singular governance. When multiple hands are involved, progress slows and tension rises. Competing hands look like shared decision-making without clear authority. It can happen in situations where a person accepts financial "help" that comes with influence or control. This can happen when obligations are formed without consent. Pressure disguised as generosity is another pathway. When access is granted during a crisis, but things never get back to normal, or you *never can pay that person back.*

No one may intend to control, but control emerges because jurisdiction that was relinquished, usually for a financial emergency was never reclaimed.

Financial ENTANGLEMENTS may Form when a person may accept assistance during hardship. They may defer decisions to keep peace. They may give power of attorney or allow someone else to "handle" finances temporarily. They could prioritize another's comfort over clarity, making ill-advised loans. Those are normal ways, but there are other deeper, darker ways.

You pay money into an altar, even a Godly altar at church. Anything you do with repetition and regularity is "religion." You go to a church, and you put money on that altar, then there is an expectation that you will continue to do that. Any person that you give money to – are they an *altar*? You only need to worry if it is not a Godly altar. If it is an evil altar, it will follow you and try to punish you if you do not continue the worship, no matter what kind of worship it was. Any altar not sanctioned by God is an evil altar.

Families that trade money back and forth all day long create financial entanglements.

At first, this feels like relief, but over time choices narrow, options require permission, movement slows, anxiety increases. Money is not in and of itself evil, as some people believe and have been taught, but the lust for money is where evil comes in. but when authority is divided, Finances cannot move properly. Competing hands is divided governance that can slow money flow to a trickle or cut it off completely.

You ever have a boyfriend (or girlfriend) and money seems a little slow until after you break up with them? Then all of a sudden people who wouldn't help you or give you a dime before are now so generous with you. Yes, you think it's because they didn't like your friend, or because you had a friend and that friend should be helping you. It could be all that, but when we look in the spirit realm we will see more truth.

Jurisdiction over the money in your hands was unclear. That happens when every decision requires negotiation, when growth creates conflict, when progress feels disloyal, and when independence feels risky. If the person that you are associated with is not self-governed, but instead they are over-governed that affects you in many ways and one of those ways can be your finances.

That is the cost of competing hands. Jurisdictional entanglement: when you've given authority over to people who shouldn't have it, this is competing hands.

If you can say that you did not give up authority on purpose, but maybe you at some time in life allowed it to remain unclaimed, then you are on your way to solving this problem. Unintentional surrender is not failure. It is unexamined access, and once noticed, it can be corrected. This is a good place to look in the spirit and be very prayerful to be sure that you are not entangled in a way that you would not even suspect. Maybe looking at your finances is the first clue. I remind you, it is known on deliverance ground that *spirit spouse* drains **money** from its victims. So you get rid of it and the competing hands issue is abated and your money will flow to you and not away from you again.

GOD DOES NOT BLESS DIVIDED JURISDICTION. God's provision restores **agency**, not dependency.

When finances are entangled obedience is delayed. Generosity is compromised. movement is restrained. God does not advance life where authority is fragmented. Two are not walking together if she wants to tithe and he doesn't. Or, if she wants to give offerings and he wants to go to clubs and drink. How can God bless the money in that marriage? In that house?

> Where the people is one, there God commands the blessing.

Life requires direction. Money likes a husband and a wife the most. (sorry singles), but only if that married couple is on one accord. Where more than one hand governs, life slows. Why? Because authority is divided. God supplies provision, but He honors jurisdiction.

Many people pray for financial breakthrough when what they actually need is jurisdictional clarity. Money flows best where it is governed. No illegal knot survives once authority is reclaimed.

Money. Order. It will flow.

ENTANGLEMENTS IN LEADERSHIP & MINISTRY

Leadership and ministry are fertile ground for entanglement because leaders can be accessible spiritually, emotionally, energetically, prayer-wise, and prophetically.

We will talk more about that later, but entanglements can happen when people are unhealed, unanchored, lonely, broken, aimless, or spiritually porous themselves. This means that folk who don't have spiritual walls up can be easy targets and victims. No walls up means no established boundaries. It could mean they are nice people, even Christians but they have no or a compromised prayer life; no walls.

Leaders. especially spiritually gifted ones, often do not realize your presence becomes a gravitational field; the anointing draws. People orbit you without permission. People tie into you without covenant. People place you in roles God never assigned. People on assignment against you will show up. You don't have to go looking for the devil for him or a representative to show up. Did Eve look for the Serpent? Scripture doesn't say so. Seems the Serpent found Eve.

If one anointed of God doesn't understand the mechanics of entanglements, they can become knotted by the very people you're called to help. Eve became entangled and it affected first herself, then Adam, then all of mankind. Then Jesus had to come and buy us back.

The "soft spot" of spiritual leadership is that the pastor or other leader can have a heart for people that is or can become a knot.

Leaders have compassion, empathy, spiritual weight-bearing capacity, patience, tolerance, a healing presence, and often a stabilizing presence. These qualities make them an anchor for others. These same qualities can make a person a magnet and especially since they are anointed of God and anointing draws, but they can also make you a magnet.

Broken people often just naturally tie themselves into strong people, though not always intentionally. The danger is when someone attaches themselves to your stability, you may begin to feel responsible for their instability. This responsibility becomes a thread. A thread becomes a knot. And a knot becomes a drain. If there is a person who is drowning but you jump in to save them, if you are not supposed to be saving them in the way you think they should be saved, or the way they want to be saved, that's danger. If you have not been sent of God with the right kind of anointing and enough of it to save them—that unsanctioned Mercy could have tied a most dangerous knot.

Those with congregations are susceptible to congregational entanglements. They see you as pastor, healer, leader, therapist, and prophet — all at once. And if you've decided that you are their parent – well, we've talked about that already. People project onto leaders for their unmet needs, their past wounds and unhealed hurts. They may tie themselves on for their spiritual expectations, desire for emotional safety, their longing for identity, and their hunger for guidance. When projection meets influence, a knot forms.

Signs of congregational entanglement are as follows. They react personally to your boundaries. they interpret ministry decisions emotionally. They expect access beyond your role. They want spiritual intimacy without spiritual maturity. They take your distance as rejection. they read into your silence. they want a connection you didn't consent to. This is not covenant. Nor is it mentoring. This is not relationship. It is spiritual dependency disguised as devotion.

Moses sat to judge the people day and night and Jethro suggested he get help. Jethro addressed in Exodus 18 was the *risk and reality of leadership entanglement*—even though Scripture doesn't use that modern term.

Moses sits "to judge the people from morning unto evening. (Exodus 18:13-26)

Jethro observes and says (paraphrased): *What you are doing is not good. You will surely wear away. This thing is too heavy for you. You are not able to perform it alone.*

1. Relational entanglement will lead to fatigue and structural overload. Moses was becoming personally entangled in every dispute. every grievance, every conflict. every emotional tension. Instead of leading *from above*, he was being pulled *into* the emotional lives of the people. That is a classic leadership entanglement when a leader becomes the *container* for everyone else's unresolved issues.

2. Emotional & Cognitive Entanglement. The phrase *"you will surely wear away"* (Exod. 18:18) implies mental exhaustion. emotional depletion, diminished discernment over time.

This is what happens when too many human burdens braid themselves into one leader's soul. Jethro doesn't say Moses is sinful. He says the *load is wrong*.

3. Authority Entanglement. Moses was functioning as prophet, judge, mediator, counselor, decision-maker, spiritual authority. All at once. That concentration of authority creates entanglement risk, blurred boundaries, dependency, bottlenecked wisdom, unhealthy emotional reliance on the leader.

Jethro's solution is delegation, not because Moses lacked calling, but because calling without structure entangles the leader. Jethro's Insight Was Structural, Not

Merely Practical. Jethro doesn't say, "Work fewer hours" "Care less" "Lower standards" He says, *"Provide out of all the people able men... and let them judge the people at all seasons."*

This separates strands, Moses → vision, law, intercession. Leaders → disputes, judgments, daily matters. That is unbraiding leadership responsibility. Moses' risk Emotional entanglement (absorbing conflict).Relational entanglement (everyone tied directly to him). Identity entanglement (indispensability). Burnout from braided responsibilities.

Jethro's solution Separation of strands. Delegation. Boundary-setting. Hierarchy. Shared burden. This is preventative unbraiding.

- Numbers 11 – Moses was overwhelmed, so God distributes the Spirit among elders
- Acts 6 – Apostles delegate to avoid neglect and burnout
- Galatians 6:5 – "Each shall bear his own load" (distinguishes shared vs. personal burden)

This shows a biblical pattern: God repeatedly unbraids leadership loads to preserve clarity and longevity. Exodus 18 provides strong biblical evidence that Jethro identified and corrected the *risk of leadership entanglement*. Not sin. Not rebellion. Not pride. But emotional overload, relational over-connection, structural imbalance. Jethro's counsel was an unbraiding strategy designed to preserve Moses, protect the people, prevent burnout, restore order.

3. THE DANGERS OF EMOTIONAL PASTORING.

"Not everyone you pastor emotionally is assigned to you spiritually." Some people are drawn to your Wisdom, empathy, warmth, clarity, authority, Peace, or presence. But emotional pastoring without boundaries creates emotional triangulation, unhealthy dependency, spiritual overreach, excessive empathy, guilt-based connections, identity entanglement.

This is when you catch yourself, thinking about them too often, worrying about their reaction, holding their emotions, carrying their spiritual progress, feeling drained, adjusting your decisions around them

This is a sign that **you are carrying emotional weight God did not assign.**

4. THE "MINISTRY FAMILY" KNOT

"People confuse family in the Spirit with family in the soul." Many spiritual leaders experience this. Someone says "You're like a mother to me." "You're my spiritual father." "You're like a sister." "You're my covering." "You feel like home."

These words feel honoring. But sometimes they're attachments disguised as affection. People can assign you an emotional or spiritual role you did not agree to. And here's the truth: The moment someone promotes you in their spirit without your permission, a thread has formed. If left unchecked, that thread becomes clinginess, offense, possessiveness, over-involvement, expectations, boundary-disrespect, and entitlement. **THE FALSE CONFIDENCE OF THE ENTANGLED.**

There is a particular category of entangled person that is especially dangerous to leaders. They appear functional. They insist they are fine. They minimize restriction. They say things such as, *"I've got this." "Don't worry about me." "I can do this and that." "Who will know?"*

This is not freedom. This is self-deception under restraint. They are not unbound — they are overextended.

This delays ministry. Entanglement does not always look like collapse. Often it looks like divided attention. A person who is bound can still show up, speak well, function, that is, perform tasks. They may be or appear committed, but they cannot move fluidly, quickly or respond, obey immediately. Their discernment and clarity may be blurred. They often cannot leave when God says "go".

Leadership requires fluid responsiveness. God's work moves at the speed of obedience — not at the speed of accommodation, or as soon as I can, or when I get around to it.

Scriptural pattern (quiet but consistent). Throughout scripture, delay often enters through alliances, not rebellion. Abraham's call was delayed while Terah remained stationary. Abraham's movement was later complicated by lot. Moses was slowed by pharaoh who was fully entangled with his idol *gods*. It was then hindered by people who wanted Egypt *and* promise.

Saul's kingship stalled because he feared the people. Jesus repeatedly left crowds who wanted miracles without transformation. God does not argue with entanglement. He simply waits for separation.

The leaders err when they delay their own assignments when they believe love requires carrying everyone, patience requires tolerating restriction, loyalty requires ignoring knots, unity requires silence.

Scripture never defines unity as braiding what God is unbraiding or leaning onto one's own understanding as to what to braid and when to leave off braiding.

You cannot move into a new season while remaining in alliance with people committed to the old one. Movement requires alignment.

How can two walk together unless they be agreed?
(Amos 3)

"Who will know?" is the wrong question. Entanglement that remains in place will ask, if i keep doing this, (while i do the other thing), *"who will know?"* Authority always asks, "who authorized this?"

God does not bless hidden restriction. He does not advance purpose through divided governance. What is concealed from people is never concealed from heaven.

When separation is required it may not always mean cutting people off. It could simply mean redefining roles, releasing responsibility, refusing emotional regulation, guilt trips and mind games. Ending compensatory behavior, declining partnership without freedom.

But it means a leader may not carry what God is requiring someone else to confront. Entangled people do not stop ministries — they slow them until obedience becomes unavoidable. God does not advance leaders through alliances that contradict freedom.

Leadership requires movement. Entanglement resists movement. Tin man? Without the Grace of the anointing, even gifts are not empowered to work and flow. When leaders tolerate knots either in themselves or others, they may not lose calling. They lose momentum. God, who governs life, will not hurry what is restrained.

This is the "spiritual family knot."

Ministry "Mothership" Syndrome, *"Leaders often attract people who want to be carried instead of grown."* When you carry people who refuse to carry themselves, the cord becomes heavy. You start to feel fatigued, overwhelmed obligated, emotionally taxed, spiritually drained, and distracted from your calling.

This is not compassion, This is soul piracy — emotional burdens hitchhiking on your anointing.

You're not supposed to mother the whole church. You're not supposed to father every wounded believer. You're not supposed to rescue every broken soul. Compassion without boundaries creates entanglement.

Leaders, peers, co-workers, discern spirits, vet people very well. Do not tie yourself to people who are otherwise already tied…

PROPHETIC ENTANGLEMENT

Balance is key, because if that weren't enough, too much spiritual transparency creates knots. Prophets often reveal too much, pour too deeply connect too spiritually carry too sensitively intercede too long, empathize too intensely.

This creates invisible spiritual bonds with people who were never meant to have emotional or spiritual access to you. Prophetic entanglements sound like: "I keep dreaming about them." "I feel their emotions." "I sense their atmosphere." "I feel guilty when they're struggling." "I can't shake them spiritually." This is not prophetic burden — this is prophetic entanglement. Prophets must learn to feel without absorbing, discern without carrying, and sense without merging.

Entanglement through serving *"Just because they serve you doesn't mean they belong to your inner court."* Entanglements form with armor bearers, ministry assistants, prayer partners, mentees, volunteers, spiritual sons and daughters, people who admire your gift.

This happens when proximity becomes unhealthy closeness, familiarity becomes emotional merging, respect becomes emotional attachment, serving becomes access, loyalty becomes dependency.

When someone ties their identity to **your** role, the knot becomes spiritual.

People with strong mercy tendencies are often vulnerable to entanglement because they feel deeply and move quickly toward the needs of others. Having a strong Our God is full of Mercy, so having a Mercy gift does not mean you don't have discernment. Mercy doesn't lack discernment; but due to compassion, it often refuses to enforce it.

When God does that, don't we call that ***Grace***?

People with strong prophetic or black-and-white tendencies are vulnerable because they see deeply and move quickly toward perceived purpose in others. One is pulled in through empathy, the other through discernment. In both cases, gifting becomes an opening when it operates without boundaries.

I renounce every invisible knot in my spirit.
Every emotional thread, spiritual thread, mental thread,
dream thread, identity thread —
loose me now.
I was not created to live constricted.
I was created to live clear. I was created to live free.
I return to myself.
And every knot begins to loosen, to unbraid.

In the Name of Jesus, Amen.

WHEN THE LEADER IS ENTANGLED

Even strong leaders can get knotted by the wrong connection. Leaders get entangled when: someone mirrors their woundedness, someone offers admiration, someone provides emotional refuge, someone "understands them", someone partners with their vulnerability, someone fills a leadership loneliness gap, someone spiritually mimics them, someone offers affirmation they don't receive elsewhere.

Leaders are human; humanity is where knots form. And the enemy knows: If he can knot the leader, he can knot the ministry. If he can knot the ministry, he can knot the assignment. Feed my sheep. Prepare for Me a people…

This is why leadership entanglements are so spiritually violent. They affect discernment, direction, relationships, decision-making, integrity, emotional stability, prophetic clarity. You are not weak because you were entangled. Leadership or other relationship or connection, know this: You were targeted for entanglement because you've got what God gave you and it is desirable, and You are not weak; you are strong.

Dear Reader

Thank you for acquiring and reading this book, I pray it has blessed you to understand entanglements of every kind and begin to take the steps to deliverance from them. The next book in this series is: **Into Freedom from Entanglements.**

Shalom,

Dr. Marlene Miles

Prayerbooks by this author

There are some books that are only prayers. You just open up the book and pray.

Prayers Against Barrenness: *For Success in Business and Life*

Fruit of the Womb: *Prayers Against Barrenness*

Beauty Curses, *Warfare Prayers Against*
https://a.co/d/5Xlc20M

Courts of Marriage: Prayers for Marriage in the Courts of Heaven *(prayerbook)* https://a.co/d/cNAdgAq

Courtroom Warfare @ Midnight *(prayerbook)*
https://a.co/d/5fc7Qdp

Demonic Cobwebs *(prayerbook)* https://a.co/d/fp9Oa2H

Every Evil Bird https://a.co/d/hF1kh1O

Gates of Thanksgiving

Spirits of Death, Hell & the Grave, Pass Over Me and My House

Throne of Grace: Courtroom Prayer

Warfare Prayer Against Poverty
https://a.co/d/bZ611Yu

Prayer Manuals

FAKE FRIENDS: *Prayers Against Betrayers*

HOLIDAY WARFARE Prayer Manual (humorous) Surviving Family Gatherings All Year Long (without catching a case)

SOUL TIE Prayer Manual (The)   Part of a 3-part series including a workbook.

MAD at DADDY Prayer Manual – part of a 3-part series including a workbook.

Healing the Sibling & Relative Wound Prayer Manual

Healing the Father-Son Wound Prayer Manual

Prayers Against Barrenness: *For Success in Business and Life*

Breaking Curses of the Mother Prayer Manual

Other books by this author

Abundance of Jesus (The) https://a.co/d/5gHJVed

AK: The Adventures of the Agape Kid

Already Married in the Spirit: *Why You May Not Be Married in the Natural*

AMONG SOME THIEVES https://a.co/d/dkYT4ZV

Ancestral Powers

Anti-Marriage, *The Spirit of*

Backstabbers https://a.co/d/gi8iBxf

Barrenness, *Prayers Against* https://a.co/d/feUltIs

Battlefield of Marriage, *The*

Beware of the Dog: Prayers Against Dogs in the Dream.

Bless Your Food: *Let the Dining Table be Undefiled*
https://a.co/d/6oPMRDv

Blindsided: *Has the Old Man Bewitched You?*
https://a.co/d/5O2fLLR

Break Free from Collective Captivity

Broken Spirits & Dry Bones

By Means of a Whorish Father

Caged Life: Get Out Alive! https://a.co/d/bwPbksX

Casting Down Imaginations

Christ of God (*The*) 3-book series

Christ of God, (*The*) Box Set, includes all three books

Churchzilla, The Wanna-Be, Supposed-to-be Bride of Christ https://a.co/d/eAf5j3x

Collateral Damage: *When What Happened Spiritually Was Your Fault*

Demonic Cobwebs (prayerbook)

Demonic Time Bombs

Demons Hate Questions

Devil Loves Trauma, *The*

Devil Weapons: Unforgiveness, Bitterness,…

The Devourers: Thieves of Darkness 2

Do Not Swear by the Moon

Don't Refuse Me, Lord (4 book series)
https://a.co/d/idP34LG

Dream Defilement

The Emptiers: *Thieves of Darkness, 1*
https://a.co/d/5I4n5mc

Evil Touch

Failed Assignment

Fantasy Spirit Spouse https://a.co/d/hW7oYbX

FAT Demons (The): *Breaking Demonic Curses*
https://a.co/d/4kP8wV1

The Fold (5-book series)

- The Fold (Book 1)
- Name Your Seed (Book 2)
- The Poor Attitudes of Money (3)
- Do Not Orphan Your Seed (4)
- For the Sake of the Gospel (5)
- My Sowing Journal

Gang Ups: Touch Not God's Anointed

Gathered: No Longer Scattered https://a.co/d/1i5DPIX

Getting Rid of Evil Spiritual Food

https://a.co/d/i2L3WYQ

got HEALING? Verses for Life

got LOVE? Verses for Life https://a.co/d/8seXHPd

got HOPE? Verses for Life

got money? https://a.co/d/g2av41N

Has My Soul Been Sold? https://a.co/d/dyB8hhA

Here Come the Horns: *Skilled to Destroy* https://a.co/d/cZiNnkP

Hidden Sins: Hidden Iniquity

https://a.co/d/4Mth0wa

How to Dental Assist

How to Dental Assist2: Be Productive, Not Wasteful

How To Stay Prayed Up

How to STOP Being a Blind Witch or Warlock

I Take It Back

In Multiplying I Will Multiply Thee

Irresistible: Jesus' Triumphal Entry
https://a.co/d/dO9IfEC

KNOW YOUR BATTLE: Stop Swinging Blindly — and Win Against Opponents, Adversaries & Enemies (Workbook) https://a.co/d/eOwFKlV

Legacy

Let Me Have A Dollar's Worth
https://a.co/d/h8F8XgE

Level the Playing Field

Living for the NOW of God   https://a.co/d/6bK5duE

Lose My Location https://a.co/d/crD6mV9

Love Breaks Your Heart

Mad At Daddy: Healing Father-Wounds that Affect Motherhood (book, workbook & prayer manual)

Made Perfect In Love

Mammon https://a.co/d/29yhMG7

Man Safari, *The*

Marriage Ed.: *Rules of Engagement & Marriage*

Made Perfect in Love

Money Hunters: Beware of Those

Money on the Altar https://a.co/d/4EqJ2Nr

Mulberry Tree, *The* https://a.co/d/9nR9rRb

Motherboard (The) - *Soul Prosperity Series*

Name Your Seed

Occupy: *Until I Return* https://a.co/d/bZ7ztUy

One Defining Day: *A Day When Dreams Come True*

Opponent, Adversary, or Enemy?: Fight The Right Battle with the Right Weapons https://a.co/d/byQqEE2 & companion workbook: Know Your Battle

Plantation Souls

Players Gonna Play

Portals: Shut the Front Door: Prayers to Close Evil Portals.

Power Money: Nine Times the Tithe

https://a.co/d/gRt41gy

The Power to Get Wealth https://a.co/d/e4ub4Ov

Powers Above

The Robe, Part 1, The Lessons of Joseph

The Robe, Part II, The Lessons of Joseph

Seasons of Grief

Seasons of Siege: God Is Coming

Seasons of Waiting

Seasons of War

Second Marriage, Third--, *Any Marriage*
https://a.co/d/6m6GN4N

Seducing Spirits: Idolatry & Whoredoms
https://a.co/d/4Jq4WEs

Shut the Front Door: *Prayers to Close Portals*
https://a.co/d/cH4TWJj

Siege: *God Is Coming*

Sift You Like Wheat

Six Men Short: What Has Happened to all the Men?

SLAVE

Sleep Afflictions & Really Bad Dreams
https://a.co/d/f8sDmgv

Soul Prosperity soul prosperity series 3

https://a.co/d/5p8YvCN

Soul Ties: How Soul Ties Form, and How To Break Them (book, workbook & prayer manual)

Souls In Captivity

The Spirit of Anti-Marriage

The Spirit of Poverty https://a.co/d/abV2o2e

Spiritual Thieves https://a.co/d/eqPPz33

StarStruck- Triangular Power series.

SUNBLOCK- Triangular Power series.

The Swallowers: *Thieves of Darkness*, 3

Take It Back

This Is NOT That: How to Keep Demons from Coming at You

Time Is of the Essence

Too Many Wives: *Why You Have Lady Problems*

Tormenting Spirits   https://a.co/d/dAogEJf

Toxic Souls

Triangular Power *(series),* Powers Above, SUNBLOCK, Do Not Swear by the Moon, STARSTRUCK

TRIBE: *What Covenants Are Governing You…?*

Unbreak My Heart: *Don't Let Me Die*

Uncontested Doom

Ungoverned Hunger: How Unchecked Appetite Dismantles Authority

Unguarded Hours, *The*

Unseen Life, *The* (forthcoming)

Upgrade: How to Get Out of Survival Mode   Toxic Souls (Book 2 of series) , Legacy (Book 3 of series)

The Wasters: *Thieves of Darkness*, Bk 2
https://a.co/d/bUvI9Jo

What Have You to Declare? What Do You Have With You from Where You've Been?

When I Was A Child, *I Prayed As a Child*

When the Devourer is Rebuked https://a.co/d/1HVv8oq

When The Table Is Set Against You

WTH? Get Me Out of This Hell
https://a.co/d/a7WBGJh

The Wilderness Romance *(series)* This series is about conducting a Godly relationship and marriage with someone who is a Wilderness person. *The Social Wilderness*

- *The Sexual Wilderness*
- *The Spiritual Wilderness*

Other Series

The Fold (a series on Godly finances) https://a.co/d/4hz3unj

Soul Prosperity Series https://a.co/d/bz2M42q

Spirit Spouse books

https://a.co/d/9VehDSo

https://a.co/d/97sKOwm

Battlefield of Marriage, The

https://a.co/d/eUDzizO

Players Gonna Play

https://a.co/d/2hzGw3N

Sent Spirit Spouse (can someone send you a spirit spouse? This book is not yet released.)

Matters of the Heart, Made Perfect in Love
https://a.co/d/70MQW3O , Love Breaks Your Heart
https://a.co/d/4KvuQLZ, Unbreak My Heart
https://a.co/d/84ceZ6M Broken Spirits & Dry Bones
https://a.co/d/e6iedNP

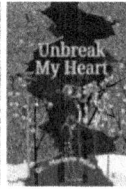

Thieves of Darkness series

The Emptiers https://a.co/d/heio0dO

The Wasters https://a.co/d/5TG1iNQ

The Swallowers https://a.co/d/1jWhM6G

The Devourers: Why We Can't Have Nice Things
https://a.co/d/87Tejbf

Spiritual Thieves

Red Flags: The Track Is Not Safe (book & workbook)

Triangular Powers https://a.co/d/aUCjAWC

Upgrade (series) *How to Get Out of Survival Mode*
https://a.co/d/aTERhXO

We Get Along, Right? Compatibility for Couples – (book & workbook)

Dr. Marlene Miles is a teacher, author, and spiritual thinker known for her grounded, discerning approach to prayer and spiritual formation. Her work emphasizes clarity, restraint, and maturity in faith—helping believers move beyond emotionalism and performance into a steady, practiced walk with God.

With a deep respect for Scripture and a practical understanding of daily life, Dr. Miles writes for those who want their prayer life to be formed, not dramatized. Her teaching encourages spiritual maintenance, discernment, and responsibility—so faith remains strong not only in crisis, but in everyday living.

www.ingramcontent.com/pod-product-compliance
Lightning Source LLC
Chambersburg PA
CBHW070156100426
42743CB00013B/2935